GREATEST EVER
Chocolate

This is a Papplewick Press Book
First published in 2002

Papplewick Press
Unit 5 Bestwood Business Park
Bestwood Village
Nottingham NG6 8AN, UK

Copyright © Parragon 2002

All rights reserved. No part of this publication may be reproduced, stored
in a retrieval system or transmitted, in any form or by any means, electronic,
mechanical, photocopying, recording or otherwise, without the prior permission
of the copyright holder.

ISBN: 0-75259-334-X

Printed in Dubai

NOTE

This book uses metric and imperial measurements. Follow the same units
of measurement throughout; do not mix metric and imperial.
All spoon measurements are level: teaspoons are assumed to be 5 ml,
and tablespoons are assumed to be 15 ml. Unless otherwise stated,
milk is assumed to be full fat, eggs and individual vegetables such as potatoes
are medium, and pepper is freshly ground black pepper.

Recipes using raw or very lightly cooked eggs should be
avoided by infants, the elderly, pregnant women, convalescents, and anyone
suffering from an illness.

Contents

Introduction   4

Basic Recipes   6

Cakes, Gâteaux & Loaves   8

Hot Desserts   62

Cold Desserts   106

Small Cakes & Cookies   172

Sweets & Drinks   224

Index   254

Introduction

Chocolate! The mere mention of anything associated with this mouthwatering confection can cause a dreamy look to come into the eyes of the chocoholic.

The cocoa tree, Theobroma cacao, originated in South America, and from the early 7th century it was cultivated by the Maya, who established a flourishing trade and even used the cocoa bean as currency. In 1502, Christopher Columbus took the cocoa bean to Spain, but it wasn't until later that Cortés introduced xocotlatl, a recipe brought from the Mexican court of Montezuma for a drink made of crushed roasted cocoa beans and cold water. Vanilla, spices, honey and sugar were added to improve the flavour of this thick and bitter brew, and over time it came to be served hot. Cocoa was believed to cure a variety of physical illnesses, and to promote stamina.

In the 17th century, the popularity of cocoa spread to the rest of Europe. France was the first country to fall to its charms, then Holland, where Amsterdam became the most important cocoa port beyond Spain. From there cocoa went to Germany, then north to Scandinavia, and also south to Italy.

Cocoa arrived in England in the mid-17th century, and chocolate houses quickly began to rival the newly established coffee houses.

In the early 19th century, Dutch chemist Coenraad Van Houten invented a press to extract the fat from the beans, and developed a method of neutralising the acids. In this way, he was able to produce almost pure cocoa butter and a hard 'cake', which could be milled to a powder for use as a flavouring. As a result, it became possible to eat chocolate as well as to drink it.

In Britain, Fry's chocolate appeared in 1847, and in Switzerland the famous chocolate companies were established. In 1875 chocolate was combined with condensed milk to produce the first milk chocolate. At around this time, Lindt found a way of making the smooth, melting chocolate still associated with the company today.

Cocoa trees are grown in Africa, the West Indies, the tropical areas of Americas, and the Far East. Harvested cocoa beans are left in the heat of the sun to develop their chocolate flavour, then afterwards the beans are shelled and the kernels are processed to produce cocoa solids. Finally, the cocoa butter is extracted and further processed to become chocolate, in all its many guises.

Basic Recipes

Preparing Chocolate

To melt chocolate on the hob:

1 Break the chocolate into small, equal-sized pieces and put it into a heatproof bowl.

2 Place the bowl over a pan of hot, simmering water, making sure the base of the bowl does not come into contact with the water.

3 Once the chocolate begins to melt, stir gently until smooth, then remove from the heat.

Note: Do not melt chocolate over direct heat (unless melting with other ingredients – in this case, keep the heat very low).

To melt chocolate in a microwave oven:

1 Break the chocolate into small pieces and place in a microwave-proof bowl.

2 Put the bowl in the microwave oven and melt. As a guide, melt 125 g/4½ oz plain chocolate on High for 2 minutes, and white or milk chocolate on Medium for 2–3 minutes.

Note: As microwave oven temperatures and settings vary, you should consult the manufacturer's instructions first.

3 Stir the chocolate with a spoon, leave to stand for a few minutes, then stir again. If necessary, return it to the microwave for a further 30 seconds.

Chocolate Decorations

Decorations add a special touch to a cake or dessert. They can be interleaved with non-stick baking paper and stored in airtight containers. Plain chocolate will keep for 4 weeks, and milk or white chocolate for 2 weeks.

Caraque

1 Spread the melted chocolate over a clean acrylic chopping board and leave it to set.

2 When the chocolate has set, hold the board firmly, position a large, smooth-bladed knife on the chocolate and pull the blade towards you at an angle of 45°, scraping along the chocolate to form the caraque. You should end up with irregularly shaped long curls.

3 Using the knife blade, lift the caraque off the board.

Quick Curls

1 For quick curls, choose a thick bar of chocolate, and keep it at room temperature.

2 Using a sharp, swivel-bladed vegetable peeler, scrape lightly along the chocolate to form fine curls, or more firmly to form thicker curls.

Note: Before grating chocolate, make sure the chocolate is firm. In warm weather, chill the chocolate in the refrigerator before using.

Leaves

1 Use freshly picked leaves with well-defined veins that are clean, dry and pliable. Holding a leaf by its stem, paint a smooth layer of melted chocolate onto the underside with a small paint brush or pastry brush.

2 Repeat with the remaining leaves, then place them, chocolate-side up, on a baking sheet lined with greaseproof paper.

3 Leave to chill for at least 1 hour until set. When set, peel each leaf away from its chocolate coating.

Cakes, Gâteaux & Loaves

It is hard to resist the pleasure of a sumptuous piece of chocolate cake and no chocolate book would be complete without a selection of cakes, gâteaux and loaves – there are plenty to choose from in this chapter. The more experimental amongst you can vary the fillings or decorations according to what takes your fancy. Alternatively, follow our easy step-by-step instructions and look at our glossy pictures to guide you to perfect results.

The gâteaux in this book are a feast for the eyes, and so are the delicious cakes, many of which can be made with surprising ease. The loaves are the perfect indulgence for teatime and can be made with very little effort. So next time you feel like a mouthwatering slice of something, these recipes are sure to be a success.

chocolate almond cake

serves eight

175 g/6 oz plain chocolate

175 g/6 oz butter

125 g/4½ oz caster sugar

4 eggs, separated

¼ tsp cream of tartar

6 tbsp self-raising flour

125 g/4½ oz ground almonds

1 tsp almond essence

TOPPING

125 g/4½ oz milk chocolate

25 g/1 oz butter

4 tbsp double cream

TO DECORATE

25 g/1 oz toasted flaked almonds

25 g/1 oz plain chocolate, melted

1 Lightly grease and line the base of a 23-cm/9-inch round springform cake tin. Break the chocolate into small pieces and place in a small saucepan with the butter. Heat gently, stirring until melted and well combined.

2 Place 100 g/3½ oz of the caster sugar in a bowl with the egg yolks and whisk until pale and creamy. Add the melted chocolate mixture, beating until well combined.

3 Sift the cream of tartar and flour together and fold into the chocolate mixture with the ground almonds and almond essence.

4 Whisk the egg whites in a bowl until standing in soft peaks. Add the remaining caster sugar and whisk for 2 minutes by hand, or 45–60 seconds, if using an electric mixer, until thick and glossy. Fold the egg whites

into the chocolate mixture and spoon into the prepared tin. Bake in a preheated oven, 190°C/375°F/Gas Mark 5, for 40 minutes, until just springy to the touch. Leave to cool.

5 Heat the topping ingredients in a bowl over a pan of hot water. Remove from the heat and beat for 2 minutes. Leave to cool for 30 minutes. Transfer the cake to a plate and spread with the topping. Scatter with the almonds and drizzle with melted chocolate. Leave to set for 2 hours before serving.

chocolate tray bake

serves fifteen

350 g/12 oz self-raising flour, sifted

3 tbsp cocoa powder, sifted

225 g/8 oz caster sugar

225 g/8 oz soft margarine,
   plus extra for greasing

4 eggs, beaten

4 tbsp milk

50 g/1¾ oz milk chocolate chips

50 g/1¾ oz plain chocolate chips

50 g/1¾ oz white chocolate chips

VARIATION

For an attractive finish, cut thin strips of paper and lay them in a criss-cross pattern across the top of the cake. Dust with icing sugar, then remove the paper strips.

---

3 Beat in the milk, plain and white chocolate chips.

4 Spoon the mixture into the prepared cake tin and smooth the top. Bake in a preheated oven, 180°C/350°F/Gas Mark 4, for 30–40 minutes, until risen and springy to the touch. Leave to cool in the tin.

5 Once cool, dust with icing sugar. Cut into squares to serve.

1 Grease a 33 x 23 x 5-cm/13 x 9 x 2-inch cake tin with a little butter or margarine.

2 Place all of the ingredients except for the chocolate chips and icing sugar in a large mixing bowl and beat together until smooth.

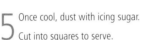

chocolate & pineapple cake

serves nine

150 g/5½ oz low-fat spread

125 g/4½ oz caster sugar

100 g/3½ oz self-raising flour, sifted

3 tbsp cocoa powder, sifted

1½ tsp baking powder

2 eggs

225 g/8 oz canned unsweetened
   pineapple pieces in fruit juice

125 ml /4 fl oz low-fat thick natural
   yogurt

about 1 tbsp icing sugar

grated chocolate, to decorate

COOK'S TIP

Store the cake, undecorated,
in an airtight container
for up to 3 days. Once
decorated, refrigerate and
use within 2 days.

1 Lightly grease a 20-cm/8-inch square cake tin.

2 Place the low-fat spread, caster sugar, flour, cocoa powder, baking powder and eggs in a large mixing bowl. Beat with a wooden spoon or electric mixer until smooth.

3 Pour the cake mixture into the prepared tin and smooth the surface. Bake in a preheated oven, 190°C/325°F/Gas Mark 5, for 20–25 minutes or until springy to the touch. Leave the cake to cool slightly in the tin before transferring to a wire rack to cool completely.

4 Drain the pineapple, chop the pineapple pieces and drain again. Reserve a little pineapple for decoration, then stir the rest into the yogurt and sweeten to taste with icing sugar.

5 Using a palette knife, spread the pineapple and yogurt mixture smoothly and evenly over the cake and decorate with the reserved pineapple pieces. Sprinkle with the grated chocolate.

family chocolate cake

serves eight

125 g/4½ oz soft margarine

125 g/4½ oz caster sugar

2 eggs

1 tbsp golden syrup

125 g/4½ oz self-raising flour, sifted

2 tbsp cocoa powder, sifted

FILLING AND TOPPING

50 g/1¾ oz icing sugar, sifted

25 g/1 oz butter

100 g/3½ oz white or milk cooking
chocolate

a little milk or white chocolate,
melted (optional)

1 Lightly grease two 18-cm/7-inch shallow cake tins.

2 Place all of the ingredients for the cake in a large mixing bowl and beat with a wooden spoon or electric mixer to form a smooth mixture.

3 Divide the mixture between the prepared tins and smooth the tops. Bake in a preheated oven, 190°C/375°F/Gas Mark 5, for 20 minutes or until springy to the touch. Cool for a few minutes in the tins before transferring to a wire rack to cool completely.

4 To make the filling, beat the icing sugar and butter together in a bowl until light and fluffy. Melt the cooking chocolate and beat half into the icing mixture. Use the filling to sandwich the 2 cakes together.

5 Spread the remaining melted cooking chocolate over the top of the cake. Pipe circles of contrasting melted milk or white chocolate and feather into the cooking chocolate with a cocktail stick, if liked. Leave to set before serving.

chocolate & orange cake

serves eight

175 g/6 oz caster sugar

175 g/6 oz butter or block
  margarine

3 eggs, beaten

175 g/6 oz self-raising flour, sifted

2 tbsp cocoa powder, sifted

2 tbsp milk

3 tbsp orange juice

grated rind of ½ orange

ICING

175 g/6 oz icing sugar

2 tbsp orange juice

a little melted chocolate

VARIATION

Add 2 tablespoons of rum or brandy to the chocolate mixture instead of the milk. The cake also works well when flavoured with grated lemon rind and juice instead of the orange.

---

1 Lightly grease a 20-cm/8-inch deep round cake tin.

2 Beat the sugar and butter or margarine together in a bowl until light and fluffy. Gradually add the eggs, beating well after each addition. Carefully fold in the flour.

3 Divide the cake mixture in half. Add the cocoa powder and milk to one half, stirring until well combined. Flavour the other half of the mixture with the orange juice and rind.

4 Place spoonfuls of each mixture into the prepared tin and swirl together with a skewer, to create a marbled effect. Bake in a preheated oven, 190°C/375°F/Gas Mark 5, for 25 minutes or until springy to the touch.

5 Leave the cake to cool in the tin for a few minutes, then transfer to a wire rack and leave to cool completely.

6 To make the icing, sift the icing sugar into a mixing bowl and mix in enough of the orange juice to form a smooth icing. Spread the icing over the top of the cake and leave to set. Pipe fine lines of melted chocolate in a decorated pattern over the top.

mocha layer cake

serves eight

200 g/7 oz self-raising flour

¼ tsp baking powder

4 tbsp cocoa powder

100 g/3½ oz caster sugar

2 eggs

2 tbsp golden syrup

150 ml/5 fl oz sunflower oil

150 ml/5 fl oz milk

FILLING

1 tsp instant coffee powder

1 tbsp boiling water

300 ml/10 fl oz double cream

2 tbsp icing sugar

TO DECORATE

50 g/1¾ oz flock chocolate

chocolate caraque (see page 7)

icing sugar, to dust

1 Lightly grease three 18-cm/7-inch cake tins.

2 Sift the flour, baking powder and cocoa powder into a large mixing bowl. Stir in the sugar. Make a well in the centre and stir in the eggs, syrup, oil and milk. Beat with a wooden spoon, gradually mixing in the dry ingredients to make a smooth batter. Divide the mixture between the prepared tins.

3 Bake in a preheated oven, 180°C/350°F/Gas Mark 4, for 35–45 minutes or until springy to the touch. Leave in the tins for 5 minutes, then turn out on to a wire rack to cool completely.

4 Dissolve the instant coffee in the boiling water and place in a bowl with the cream and icing sugar. Whip until the cream is just holding its shape. Use half of the cream to sandwich the 3 cakes together. Spread the remaining cream over the top and sides of the cake. Lightly press the flock chocolate into the cream around the edge of the cake.

5 Transfer to a serving plate. Lay the caraque over the top of the cake. Cut a few thin strips of baking paper and place on top of the caraque. Dust lightly with icing sugar, then carefully remove the paper. Serve.

devil's food cake

serves six

100 g/3½ oz plain chocolate

250 g/9 oz self-raising flour

1 tsp bicarbonate of soda

225 g/8 oz butter

400 g/14 oz dark muscovado sugar

1 tsp vanilla essence

3 eggs

125 ml/4 fl oz buttermilk

225 ml/8 fl oz boiling water

FROSTING

300 g/10½ oz caster sugar

2 egg whites

1 tbsp lemon juice

3 tbsp orange juice

candied orange peel, to decorate

COOK'S TIP

If you prefer, use a vanilla butter icing to decorate the cake. Cream 175 g/6 oz butter until soft, then add 350 g/12 oz sifted icing sugar and mix together. Stir in vanilla essence to taste. Alternatively, use whipped cream.

1 Lightly grease two 20-cm/8-inch shallow round cake tins and line the bases with baking paper. Melt the chocolate in a pan. Sift the flour and bicarbonate of soda together.

2 Beat the butter and sugar together in a bowl until pale and fluffy. Beat in the vanilla essence and the eggs, one at a time, taking care to beat well after each addition. Add a little flour to the mixture if it begins to curdle and stir well.

3 Fold the melted chocolate into the mixture until well blended. Gradually fold in the remaining flour, then gently stir in the buttermilk and boiling water.

4 Divide the mixture between the tins and smooth the tops. Bake in a preheated oven, 190°C/375°F/Gas Mark 5, for 30 minutes, until springy to the touch. Leave to cool in the tin for 5 minutes, then transfer to a wire rack and leave to cool completely.

5 Place the frosting ingredients in a large bowl set over a saucepan of gently simmering water. Whisk, preferably with an electric mixer, until thickened and forming soft peaks. Remove from the heat and whisk until the mixture is cool.

6 Sandwich the 2 cakes together with a little of the frosting, then spread the remainder over the sides and top of the cake, swirling it as you do so. Decorate the top of the cake with the candied orange peel.

chocolate tea bread

serves four

175 g/6 oz butter, softened

100 g/3½ oz light muscovado sugar

4 eggs, beaten lightly

225 g/8 oz plain chocolate chips

100 g/3½ oz raisins

50 g/1¾ oz chopped walnuts

finely grated rind of 1 orange

225 g/8 oz self-raising flour

1 Lightly grease a 900-g/2-lb loaf tin and line the base with baking paper.

2 Cream the butter and muscovado sugar together in a bowl until light and fluffy.

3 Gradually add the eggs, beating well after each addition. If the mixture begins to curdle, beat in 1–2 tablespoons of the flour.

4 Stir in the chocolate chips, raisins, walnuts and orange rind. Sift the flour and carefully fold it into the mixture.

5 Spoon the mixture into the prepared loaf tin and make a slight dip in the centre of the top with the back of a spoon.

6 Bake in a preheated oven, 160°C/325°F/Gas Mark 3, for 1 hour or until a fine skewer inserted into the centre comes out clean.

7 Leave to cool in the tin for 5 minutes, before carefully turning out and leaving on a wire rack to cool completely.

8 Serve the teabread cut into thin slices.

rich chocolate layer cake

serves ten

7 eggs

200 g/7 oz caster sugar

150 g/5½ oz plain flour

50 g/1¾ oz cocoa powder

55 g/2 oz butter, melted

FILLING

200 g/7 oz plain chocolate

125 g/4½ oz butter

4 tbsp icing sugar

TO DECORATE

75 g/2¾ oz toasted flaked almonds,
    crushed lightly

quick chocolate curls (see page 7) or
    grated chocolate

1 Grease a deep 23-cm/9-inch square cake tin and then line the base with baking paper.

2 Whisk the eggs and caster sugar together in a mixing bowl with an electric mixer for about 10 minutes or until the mixture is very light and foamy and the whisk leaves a trail that lasts a few seconds when lifted.

3 Sift the flour and cocoa together and fold half into the mixture. Drizzle over the melted butter and fold in the rest of the flour and cocoa. Pour into the tin and bake in a preheated oven, 180°C/350°F/Gas Mark 4, for 30–35 minutes or until springy to the touch. Leave to cool slightly, then remove from the tin and cool completely on a wire rack. Wash and dry the tin and return the cake to it.

4 While the cake is cooling, make the filling. Melt the plain chocolate and butter together, then remove from the heat. Stir in the icing sugar, leave to cool, then beat the filling until it is thick enough to spread.

5 Halve the cooled cake lengthways and cut each half into 3 layers. Sandwich the layers together with three-quarters of the chocolate filling. Spread the remainder over the cake and mark a wavy pattern on the top. Press the almonds on to the sides. Decorate with chocolate curls (see page 7) or grated chocolate.

chocolate passion cake

serves six

5 eggs

150 g/5½ oz caster sugar

150 g/5½ oz plain flour

40 g/1½ oz cocoa powder

175 g/6 oz carrots, peeled, grated
    finely and squeezed until dry

50 g/1¾ oz chopped walnuts

2 tbsp sunflower oil

350 g/12 oz medium-fat soft cheese

175 g/6 oz icing sugar

175 g/6 oz milk or plain chocolate,
    melted

1 Lightly grease the base of a 20-cm/8-inch deep round cake tin and line it with baking paper.

2 Place the eggs and sugar in a large mixing bowl set over a pan of gently simmering water and whisk until the mixture is thick enough to leave a trail.

3 Remove the bowl from the heat. Sift the flour and cocoa powder into the bowl and fold in. Fold in the carrots, walnuts and sunflower oil.

4 Pour into the tin and bake in a preheated oven, 190°C/375°F/ Gas Mark 5, for 45 minutes. Turn out on to a wire rack to cool completely.

5 Beat the soft cheese and icing sugar together until combined. Beat in the melted chocolate. Split the cake in half and sandwich together again with half of the chocolate mixture. Cover the top of the cake with the remainder of the chocolate mixture, swirling it with a knife. Leave to chill or serve immediately.

chocolate yogurt cake

serves eight

150 ml/5 fl oz vegetable oil

150 ml/5 fl oz whole-milk natural
   yogurt

175 g/6 oz light muscovado sugar

3 eggs, beaten

100 g/3½ oz wholemeal self-raising
   flour

125 g/4½ oz self-raising flour, sifted

2 tbsp cocoa powder

1 tsp bicarbonate of soda

50 g/1¾ oz plain chocolate, melted

FILLING AND TOPPING

150 ml/5 fl oz whole-milk natural
   yogurt

150 ml/5 fl oz double cream

225 g/8 oz fresh soft fruit, such as
   strawberries or raspberries

1 Grease a deep 23-cm/9-inch
   round cake tin and line the base
with baking paper.

2 Place the oil, yogurt, sugar and
   beaten eggs in a large mixing
bowl and beat together until well
combined. Sift the flours, cocoa
powder and bicarbonate of soda
together and beat into the yogurt,

sugar and egg mixture. Beat in the
melted chocolate.

3 Pour into the prepared tin and
   bake in a preheated oven,
180°C/350°F/Gas Mark 4, for
45–50 minutes or until a fine skewer
inserted into the centre comes out
clean. Leave to cool in the tin for
5 minutes, then turn out on to a wire
rack to cool completely. When cold,
carefully split the cake into 3 layers.

4 To make the filling, place the
   yogurt and cream in a large
mixing bowl and whisk well until the
mixture stands in soft peaks.

5 Place one layer of cake on a
   serving plate and spread with
some of the cream. Top with a little
of the fruit (it is better to slice larger
fruit such as strawberries). Repeat with

the next layer. Top with the final layer
of cake and spread with the rest of the
cream. Arrange more fruit on top and
cut the cake into wedges to serve.

raspberry vacherin

serves ten

3 egg whites

175 g/6 oz caster sugar

1 tsp cornflour

25 g/1 oz plain chocolate, grated

FILLING

175 g/6 oz plain chocolate

450 ml/16 fl oz double cream,
   whipped

350 g/12 oz fresh raspberries

a little melted chocolate, to decorate

COOK'S TIP

When whisking egg whites,
make sure your bowl is spotlessly
clean and free from any grease
as the egg whites will not whisk
well and hold their shape.

1 Draw 3 rectangles, 10 x 25 cm/
4 x 10 inches, on sheets of baking
paper, and place on 2 baking trays.

2 Whisk the egg whites in a mixing
bowl until standing in soft peaks,
then gradually whisk in half of the
sugar and continue whisking until the
mixture is very stiff and glossy.

3 Carefully fold in the rest of the
sugar, the cornflour and grated
chocolate with a metal spoon.

4 Spoon the meringue mixture
into a piping bag fitted with a
1 cm/½ inch plain nozzle and pipe lines
across the baking paper rectangles.

5 Bake the meringues in a
preheated oven, 140°C/275°F/
Gas Mark 1, for 1½ hours, changing
the positions of the baking trays

halfway through cooking. Without
opening the oven door, turn off the
oven and leave the meringues inside
it to cool, then peel away the paper.

6 To make the vacherin filling, melt
the chocolate and spread it over
2 of the meringue layers. Leave to
stand until the filling has hardened.

7 Place 1 chocolate-coated
meringue on a plate and top
with about one-third of the cream and
raspberries. Gently place the second
chocolate-coated meringue on top
and spread with half of the remaining
cream and raspberries.

8 Place the last meringue on the
top and decorate it with the
remaining cream and raspberries.
Drizzle a little melted chocolate over
the top of the vacherin and serve.

sachertorte

serves ten

175 g/6 oz plain chocolate

150 g/5½ oz unsalted butter

150 g/5½ oz caster sugar

6 eggs, separated

150 g/5½ oz plain flour

ICING AND FILLING

175 g/6 oz plain chocolate

5 tbsp strong black coffee

175 g/6 oz icing sugar

6 tbsp good-quality apricot jam

50 g/1¾ oz plain chocolate,
   melted to decorate

COOK'S TIP

The finished cake is delicious
served with whipped cream
and fresh raspberries or a
raspberry coulis.

1 Grease a 23-cm/9-inch springform cake tin and line the base with baking paper. Melt the chocolate. Beat the butter and 75 g/2¾ oz of the sugar until pale and fluffy. Add the egg yolks and beat together well. Add the chocolate in a thin stream, beating well. Sift the flour and fold it into the cake mixture. Whisk the egg whites until they stand in soft peaks. Add the remaining sugar and whisk for 2 minutes by hand, or 45–60 seconds if using an electric mixer, until glossy. Fold half into the chocolate mixture, then fold in the remainder.

2 Spoon into the prepared tin and smooth the top. Bake in a preheated oven, 150°C/300°F/Gas Mark 2, for 1–1¼ hours, until a skewer inserted into the centre comes out clean. Cool in the tin for 5 minutes, then transfer to a wire rack to cool.

3 To make the icing, melt the chocolate and beat in the coffee until smooth. Sift the icing sugar into a bowl, then whisk in the melted chocolate mixture to give a thick icing. Halve the cake. Warm the jam, spread over one half of the cake and sandwich together. Invert the cake onto a wire rack. Spoon the icing over the cake and spread, as smoothly and evenly as possible, to coat the top and sides. Leave to set for 5 minutes, allowing any excess icing to drip through the rack. Transfer to a serving plate and leave to set for at least 2 hours.

4 To decorate, spoon the melted chocolate into a small piping bag and carefully pipe the word 'Sacher' or 'Sachertorte' across the top of the cake. Leave the chocolate topping to harden and set completely before serving the cake.

chocolate marshmallow cake

serves six

85 g/3 oz unsalted butter, plus
   1 tbsp for greasing

225 g/8 oz caster sugar

½ tsp vanilla essence

2 eggs, beaten lightly

85 g/3 oz plain chocolate, broken
   into pieces

150 ml/5 fl oz buttermilk

175 g/6 oz self-raising flour

½ tsp bicarbonate of soda

pinch of salt

55 g/2 oz milk chocolate, grated, to
   decorate

FROSTING

175 g/6 oz white marshmallows

1 tbsp milk

2 egg whites

2 tbsp caster sugar

1 Grease an 850-ml/1½-pint ovenproof pudding basin with butter. Cream the butter, sugar and vanilla together until very pale and fluffy, then gradually beat in the eggs.

2 Melt the plain chocolate in a heatproof bowl over a saucepan of simmering water. When the chocolate has melted, stir in the buttermilk gradually, until well combined. Remove the pan from the heat and cool slightly.

3 Sift the flour, bicarbonate of soda and salt into a separate bowl.

4 Add the chocolate mixture and the flour mixture alternately to the creamed mixture, a little at a time. Spoon the creamed mixture into the prepared basin and smooth the surface.

5 Bake in a preheated oven, 160°C/325°F/Gas Mark 3, for 50 minutes, until a skewer inserted into the centre of the cake comes out clean. Turn out on to a wire rack to cool.

6 Meanwhile, make the frosting. Put the marshmallows and milk in a small saucepan and heat very gently until the marshmallows have melted. Remove the pan from the heat and leave to cool.

7 Whisk the egg whites until soft peaks form, then add the sugar and continue whisking, until stiff peaks form. Fold the egg white into the cooled marshmallow mixture and leave to stand for 10 minutes.

8 When the cake is cool, cover the top and sides with the marshmallow frosting. Sprinkle grated milk chocolate over the frosting.

chocolate slab cake

serves ten

225 g/8 oz butter

100 g/3½ oz plain chocolate,
   chopped

150 ml/5 fl oz water

300 g/10½ oz plain flour

2 tsp baking powder

275 g/9½ oz soft brown sugar

150 ml/5 fl oz soured cream

2 eggs, beaten

FROSTING

200 g/7 oz plain chocolate

6 tbsp water

3 tbsp single cream

15 g/½ oz butter, chilled

1 Grease a 33 x 20-cm/13 x 8-inch square cake tin and line the base with baking paper. Melt the butter and chocolate with the water in a saucepan over a low heat, stirring frequently.

2 Sift the flour and baking powder into a mixing bowl and stir in the sugar. Pour the hot chocolate liquid into the bowl.

3 Beat well until all of the ingredients are evenly mixed. Stir in the soured cream, followed by the beaten eggs.

COOK'S TIP
Leave the cake on the wire rack to frost it and place a large baking tray underneath to catch any drips. Spoon any drips back on to the cake.

4 Pour the cake mixture into the prepared tin and bake in a preheated oven, 190°C/375°F/Gas Mark 5, for 40–45 minutes.

5 Leave the cake to cool in the tin before turning it out on to a wire rack. Leave to cool completely.

6 To make the frosting, melt the chocolate with the water in a saucepan over a very low heat, stir in the cream and remove from the heat. Stir in the chilled butter, then pour the frosting over the cooled cake, using a spatula to spread it evenly over the top of the cake.

mousse cake

serves twelve

175 g/6 oz butter

175 g/6 oz caster sugar

4 eggs, beaten lightly

1 tbsp cocoa powder

200 g/7 oz self-raising flour

50 g/1¾ oz plain, orange-flavoured
   chocolate, melted

ORANGE MOUSSE

2 eggs, separated

4 tbsp caster sugar

200 ml/7 fl oz freshly squeezed
   orange juice

2 tsp powdered gelatine

3 tbsp water

300 ml/10 fl oz double cream

peeled orange slices, to decorate

1 Grease a 20-cm/8-inch springform cake tin and and line the base with baking paper. Beat the butter and sugar together in a bowl until light and fluffy. Gradually add the eggs, beating well after each addition. Sift the cocoa powder and flour together and fold into the cake mixture. Fold the melted chocolate into the mixture.

2 Pour into the prepared tin and smooth the top. Bake in a preheated oven, 180°C/350°F/Gas Mark 4, for 40 minutes or until springy to the touch. Leave to cool for 5 minutes in the tin, then turn out and leave to cool completely on a wire rack. Cut the cold cake into 2 layers.

3 To make the mousse, beat the egg yolks and sugar until light, then whisk in the orange juice. Sprinkle the gelatine over the water in a small bowl and leave to go spongy, then place over a pan of hot water and stir until dissolved. Stir into the mousse.

4 Whip the cream until holding its shape, reserve a little for decoration and fold the rest into the mousse. Whisk the egg whites until standing in soft peaks, then fold in. Leave in a cool place until beginning to set, stirring occasionally.

5 Place half of the cake in the tin. Pour in the mousse and press the second cake layer on top. Chill until set. Transfer to a plate, pipe cream rosettes on the top and arrange orange slices in the centre.

chocolate roulade

serves six

150 g/5½ oz plain chocolate

2 tbsp water

6 eggs

175 g/6 oz caster sugar

3 tbsp plain flour

1 tbsp cocoa powder

FILLING

300 ml/10 fl oz double cream

75 g/2¾ oz sliced strawberries

TO DECORATE

icing sugar, for dusting

chocolate leaves (see page 7)

fresh strawberries, to serve

1 Line a 38 x 25-cm/15 x 10-inch Swiss roll tin. Melt the chocolate with the water, stirring constantly. Leave the chocolate to cool slightly.

2 Place the eggs and sugar in a bowl and whisk for 10 minutes, or until the mixture is pale and foamy and the whisk leaves a trail when lifted. Whisk in the chocolate in a thin stream. Sift the flour and cocoa powder together and fold into the mixture. Pour into the tin; smooth the top.

3 Bake in a preheated oven, 200°C/ 400°F/Gas Mark 6, for 12 minutes. Dust a sheet of baking paper with a little icing sugar. Turn out the roulade and remove the lining paper. Roll up the roulade with the fresh paper inside. Place on a wire rack, cover with a damp tea towel and leave to cool.

4 Lightly whip the cream. Unroll the roulade and scatter over the fruit. Spread three-quarters of the cream over the roulade and re-roll. Dust with icing sugar.

5 Place the roulade on a plate. Pipe the rest of the cream down the centre. Decorate with chocolate leaves and serve with fresh strawberries.

chocolate & coconut roulade

serves eight

3 eggs

75 g/2¾ oz caster sugar

5½ tbsp self-raising flour

1 tbsp block creamed coconut,
softened with 1 tbsp boiling
water

25 g/1 oz desiccated coconut

6 tbsp good-quality raspberry jam

CHOCOLATE COATING

200 g/7 oz plain chocolate

70 g/2½ oz butter

2 tbsp golden syrup

RASPBERRY COULIS

225 g/8 oz fresh or frozen
raspberries, thawed if frozen

2 tbsp water

4 tbsp icing sugar

1 Grease and line a 23 x 30-cm/
9 x 12-inch Swiss roll tin. Whisk
the eggs and caster sugar together in a
large mixing bowl with an electric
mixer for about 10 minutes, or until the
mixture is very light and foamy and the
whisk leaves a trail that lasts a few
seconds when lifted.

2 Sift the flour and fold in with
a metal spoon or a spatula. Fold
in the creamed coconut and desiccated
coconut. Pour the mixture into the
prepared tin and bake in a preheated
oven, 200°C/400°F/Gas Mark 6,
for 10–12 minutes or until springy to
the touch.

3 Sprinkle a sheet of baking paper
with a little caster sugar and place
on top of a damp tea towel. Turn the
cake out on to the paper and carefully
peel away the lining paper. Spread the
jam over the sponge and roll up from
the short end, using the tea towel to
help you. Place seam-side down on a
wire rack and leave to cool completely.

4 Meanwhile, make the coating.
Melt the chocolate and butter
together, stirring. Stir in the golden
syrup. Leave to cool for 5 minutes,
then spread it over the cooled roulade
and leave to set.

5 To make the coulis, purée the fruit
in a food processor with the water
and sugar and sieve to remove the
seeds. Cut the roulade into slices and
serve with the raspberry coulis and a
few raspberries.

chocolate brownie roulade

serves eight

150 g/5½ oz plain chocolate,
  broken into pieces

3 tbsp water

175 g/6 oz caster sugar

5 eggs, separated

25 g/1 oz raisins, chopped

25 g/1 oz pecan nuts, chopped

pinch of salt

300 ml/10 fl oz double cream,
  whipped lightly

icing sugar, for dusting

1 Grease a 30 x 20-cm/12 x 8-inch Swiss roll tin, line with baking paper and grease the paper.

2 Place the chocolate with the water in a small saucepan over a low heat, stirring until the chocolate has just melted. Leave to cool.

3 Whisk the sugar and egg yolks in a large bowl with an electric whisk for 2–3 minutes until thick and pale.

4 Fold in the cooled chocolate, raisins and pecan nuts.

5 Whisk the egg whites with the salt in a separate bowl. Fold one quarter of the egg whites into the chocolate mixture, then fold in the rest of the whites, working lightly and quickly so as not to lose any air.

6 Transfer the mixture to the prepared tin and bake in a preheated oven, 180°C/350°F/Gas Mark 4, for 25 minutes, until risen and just firm to the touch. Leave to cool before covering with a sheet of non-stick baking paper and a damp clean tea towel. Leave the roulade to stand until completely cold.

7 Turn the roulade out on to another piece of baking paper dusted with icing sugar and remove the lining paper.

8 Spread the lightly whipped cream over the roulade. Starting from a short end, roll the sponge away from you, using the paper to guide you. Trim the ends of the roulade to make a neat finish and transfer to a serving plate. Leave the roulade to chill in the refrigerator until ready to serve. Dust with a little icing sugar before serving.

almond & hazelnut gâteau

serves eight

4 eggs

100 g/3½ oz caster sugar

50 g/1¾ oz ground almonds

50 g/1¾ oz ground hazelnuts

5½ tbsp plain flour

50 g/1¾ oz flaked almonds

FILLING

100 g/3½ oz plain chocolate

15 g/½ oz butter

300 ml/10 fl oz double cream

icing sugar, for dusting

1 Grease two 18-cm/7-inch round sandwich tins and line the bases with baking paper.

2 Whisk the eggs and caster sugar together in a large mixing bowl with an electric mixer for 10 minutes or until the mixture is light and foamy and the whisk leaves a trail that lasts a few seconds when lifted.

3 Fold in the ground almonds and hazelnuts, sift the flour and fold in with a metal spoon or spatula. Pour into the prepared tins.

4 Scatter the flaked almonds over the top of one of the cakes. Bake both of the cakes in a preheated oven, 190°C/375°F/Gas Mark 5, for 15–20 minutes or until springy to the touch.

5 Leave the cakes to cool slightly in the tins. Carefully remove the cakes from the tins and transfer them to a wire rack to cool completely.

6 Meanwhile, make the filling. Melt the chocolate, remove from the heat and stir in the butter. Leave to cool slightly. Whip the cream until just holding its shape, then fold in the melted chocolate until mixed.

7 Place the cake without the extra almonds on a serving plate and spread the filling over it. Leave to set slightly, then place the almond-topped cake on top of the filling and leave to chill for about 1 hour. Dust the cake with icing sugar and serve.

layered meringue gâteau

serves eight

6 egg whites

140 g/5 oz caster sugar

175 g/6 oz icing sugar

2 tbsp cornflour

FILLING

225 ml/8 fl oz double cream

140 g/5 oz plain chocolate, broken
  into small pieces

4 tsp dark rum

TO DECORATE

150 ml/5 fl oz double cream

4 tsp caster sugar

1–2 tsp cocoa powder, for dusting

1 Prepare 5 sheets of baking paper by drawing an 18-cm/7-inch circle on each. Use them to line baking trays.

2 Whisk the egg whites until they form soft peaks. Mix the sugars and cornflour together and sift into the egg whites, a little at a time, whisking until firm peaks form.

3 Spoon the meringue mixture into a piping bag fitted with a round nozzle. Starting from the centre, carefully pipe 5 spirals, measuring 18 cm/7 inches, on each of the prepared pieces of baking paper.

4 Bake in a preheated oven, at the lowest possible temperature with the oven door kept slightly ajar, for 6 hours or overnight.

5 After baking, carefully peel the meringue spirals from the baking paper and place on wire racks to cool.

6 To make the filling, pour the cream into a pan and place over a low heat. Add the chocolate and stir until melted. Remove from the heat and beat with a hand-held whisk. Beat in the rum, then cover with clingfilm and refrigerate overnight or for as long as the meringues are in the oven.

7 To assemble the gâteau, beat the filling with an electric mixer until thick and smooth. Place 3 of the meringue layers on a work surface and spread the filling over them. Stack the 3 meringue layers, one on top of the other, and place an uncovered meringue layer on top. Crush the fifth meringue layer into crumbs.

8 To make the decoration, whip the cream with the sugar until thick. Carefully spread the mixture over the top of the gâteau. Sprinkle the meringue crumbs on top of the cream and dust the centre of the gâteau with cocoa powder. Serve within 1–2 hours.

chocolate & walnut cake

serves eight

4 eggs

125 g/4½ oz caster sugar

125 g/4½ oz plain flour

1 tbsp cocoa powder

25 g/1 oz butter, melted

75 g/2¾ oz plain chocolate, melted

150 g/5½ oz finely chopped
    walnuts

ICING

75 g/2¾ oz plain chocolate

125 g/4½ oz butter

200 g/7 oz icing sugar

2 tbsp milk

walnut halves, to decorate

1 Grease a 18-cm/7-inch deep
round cake tin and line the base.
Place the eggs and caster sugar in a
mixing bowl and whisk with electric
beaters for 10 minutes or until the
mixture is light and foamy and the
whisk leaves a trail that lasts a few
seconds when lifted.

2 Sift the flour and cocoa powder
together and fold in with a metal
spoon or spatula. Fold in the melted
butter and chocolate, and the chopped
walnuts. Pour the cake mixture into the
prepared tin and bake in a preheated
oven, 160°C/325°F/Gas Mark 3, and
bake for 30–35 minutes or until
springy to the touch.

3 Leave to cool in the tin for
5 minutes, then transfer to a wire
rack and leave to cool completely.

4 To make the icing, melt the
plain chocolate and leave to cool
slightly. Beat the butter, icing sugar and
milk together in a bowl until the
mixture is pale and fluffy. Whisk in
the melted chocolate.

5 Cut the cold cake into 2 layers.
Sandwich the 2 layers with some
of the icing and place on a serving
plate. Spread the remaining icing over
the top of the cake with a spatula,
swirling it slightly as you do so.
Decorate the cake with the walnut
halves and serve.

dobos torte

serves eight

3 eggs
100 g/3½ oz caster sugar
1 tsp vanilla essence
100 g/3½ oz plain flour
FILLING
175 g/6 oz plain chocolate
175 g/6 oz butter
2 tbsp milk
350 g/12 oz icing sugar
CARAMEL
100 g/3½ oz granulated sugar
4 tbsp water

1 Draw four 18 cm/7 inch circles on sheets of baking paper. Place 2 of them upside down on 2 baking trays.

2 Whisk the eggs and caster sugar in a large mixing bowl with an electric mixer for 10 minutes, or until the mixture is light and foamy and the whisk leaves a trail. Fold in the vanilla essence. Sift the flour and fold in with a metal spoon.

3 Spoon a one-quarter of the mixture on to one of the trays and spread out to the size of the circle. Repeat with the other circle. Bake in a preheated oven, 200°C/400°F/Gas Mark 6, for 5–8 minutes or until golden brown. Cool on wire racks. Repeat with the remaining mixture.

4 To make the filling, melt the chocolate and cool slightly. Beat the butter, milk and icing sugar until pale and fluffy. Whisk in the chocolate.

5 Place the sugar and water for the caramel in a heavy-based saucepan. Heat, stirring, to dissolve the sugar. Boil gently until pale golden in colour. Remove from the heat. Pour over one cake layer as a topping. Leave to harden slightly. Mark out 8 portions with an oiled knife.

6 Remove the cakes from the paper and trim the edges. Sandwich the layers together with some of the filling, finishing with the caramel-topped cake. Place on a serving plate, spread the sides with the filling mixture and pipe rosettes around the top.

apricot & chocolate ring

serves twelve

6 tbsp butter, diced

450 g/1 lb self-raising flour, sifted

4 tbsp caster sugar

2 eggs, beaten

150 ml/5 fl oz milk

FILLING AND DECORATION

25 g/1 oz butter, melted

150 g/5½ oz no-soak dried apricots,
   chopped

100 g/3½ oz plain chocolate chips

1–2 tbsp milk, for glazing

25 g/1 oz plain chocolate, melted

1 Grease a 25-cm/10-inch round cake tin and then line the base with baking paper.

2 Rub the butter into the flour until the mixture resembles fine breadcrumbs. Stir in the caster sugar, eggs and milk to form a soft dough.

3 Roll out the dough on a lightly floured work surface to form a 35-cm/14-inch square.

4 Brush the melted butter over the surface of the dough. Mix the apricots and chocolate chips together and, using a spoon or knife, spread them over the dough to within 2.5 cm/1 inch of the top and bottom.

5 Roll up the dough tightly, like a Swiss roll, and cut it into 2.5-cm/1-inch slices. Stand the slices in a ring around the edge of the prepared tin at a slight tilt. Brush the surface with a little milk to glaze.

6 Bake in a preheated oven, 180°C/350°F/Gas Mark 4, for 30 minutes or until cooked and golden. Leave to cool in the tin for about 15 minutes, then transfer to a wire rack to cool.

7 Drizzle the melted chocolate over the ring to decorate.

dark & white chocolate torte

serves six

4 eggs

100 g/3½ oz caster sugar

100 g/3½ oz plain flour

CHOCOLATE CREAM

300 ml/10 fl oz double cream

150 g/5½ oz plain chocolate,
    broken into small pieces

WHITE CHOCOLATE ICING

75 g/2¾ oz white chocolate

15 g/½ oz butter

1 tbsp milk

4 tbsp icing sugar

chocolate caraque (see page 7)

1 Grease a 20-cm/8-inch round springform cake tin and line the base with baking paper. Whisk the eggs and caster sugar in a large mixing bowl with an electric mixer for about 10 minutes or until the mixture is very light and foamy and the whisk leaves a trail that lasts a few seconds when lifted.

2 Sift the flour and fold in with a metal spoon or spatula. Pour into the prepared tin and bake in a preheated oven, 180°C/350°F/Gas Mark 4, for 35–40 minutes or until springy to the touch. Leave to cool

slightly, then transfer to a wire rack to cool completely.

3 To make the chocolate cream, place the cream in a saucepan and bring to the boil, stirring. Add the chocolate and stir until melted. Remove from the heat, transfer to a bowl and leave to cool. Beat with a wooden spoon until thick.

4 Cut the cold cake into 2 layers horizontally. Sandwich the layers back together with the chocolate cream and place on a wire rack.

5 To make the icing, melt the chocolate and butter together and stir until blended. Whisk in the

milk and icing sugar. Continue whisking for a few minutes until the icing is cool. Pour it over the cake and spread with a spatula to coat the top and sides. Decorate with chocolate caraque and leave to set.

bistvitny torte

serves ten

CHOCOLATE TRIANGLES

25 g/1 oz plain chocolate, melted

25 g/1 oz white chocolate, melted

CAKE

175 g/6 oz soft margarine

175 g/6 oz caster sugar

½ tsp vanilla essence

3 eggs, beaten lightly

225 g/8 oz self-raising flour

50 g/1¾ oz plain chocolate

SYRUP

125 g/4½ oz sugar

6 tbsp water

3 tbsp brandy or sherry

150 ml/5 fl oz double cream

1 Grease a 23-cm/9-inch ring tin. To make the triangles, place a sheet of baking paper on to a baking tray and place alternate spoonfuls of the dark and white chocolate on to the paper. Spread together to form a thick marbled layer. Leave to set. Cut into squares, then into triangles.

2 To make the cake, beat the margarine and sugar until light and fluffy. Beat in the vanilla essence. Gradually add the eggs, beating well after each addition. Fold in the flour. Divide the mixture in half. Melt the plain chocolate and stir into one half.

3 Place spoonfuls of each mixture into the prepared tin and swirl them together with a skewer to create a marbled effect.

4 Bake in a preheated oven, 190°C/375°F/Gas Mark 5, for 30 minutes or until the cake is springy to the touch. Leave to cool in the tin for a few minutes, then transfer to a wire rack and leave to cool completely.

5 To make the syrup, place the sugar in a small saucepan with the water and heat gently, stirring, until the sugar has dissolved. Boil gently for 1–2 minutes, then remove from the heat and stir in the brandy or sherry. Leave the syrup to cool slightly, then spoon it slowly over the cake, allowing it to soak into the sponge. Whip the cream and pipe swirls of it on top of the cake. Decorate with the chocolate triangles.

chocolate & almond torte

serves ten

225 g/8 oz plain chocolate, broken
  into pieces

3 tbsp water

150 g/5½ oz soft brown sugar

175 g/6 oz butter, softened

25 g/1 oz ground almonds

3 tbsp self-raising flour

5 eggs, separated

100 g/3½ oz blanched almonds,
  finely chopped

icing sugar, for dusting

TO SERVE

mixed fresh fruit

double cream (optional)

COOK'S TIP

For a nuttier flavour, toast
the chopped almonds in a
dry frying pan over a medium
heat for about 2 minutes
until lightly golden.

---

1 Grease a 23-cm/9-inch loose-
bottomed cake tin and line the
base with baking paper.

2 Melt the chocolate with the water,
in a saucepan set over a very low
heat, stirring until smooth. Add the
sugar and stir until thoroughly
dissolved, taking the pan off the heat
to prevent it overheating.

3 Add the butter in small amounts
until it has melted into the
chocolate. Remove from the heat and
lightly stir in the ground almonds and
flour. Add the egg yolks one at a time,
beating well after each addition.

4 In a large mixing bowl, whisk
the egg whites until they stand
in soft peaks, then fold them into the
chocolate mixture with a metal spoon.
Stir in the chopped almonds. Pour the
mixture into the prepared cake tin and
smooth the surface.

5 Bake in a preheated oven,
180°C/350°F/Gas Mark 4, for
40–45 minutes, until well risen and
firm (the cake will crack on the
surface during cooking).

6 Leave to cool in the tin for
30–40 minutes. Turn out on to
a wire rack to cool completely. Dust
with icing sugar and serve in slices
with double cream (if using).

date & chocolate cake

serves eight

115 g/4 oz plain chocolate, broken
   into pieces

1 tbsp grenadine

1 tbsp golden syrup

115 g/4 oz unsalted butter

55 g/2 oz caster sugar

2 large eggs

85 g/3 oz self-raising flour

2 tbsp ground rice

1 tbsp icing sugar, to decorate

FILLING

115 g/4 oz dried dates, chopped

1 tbsp lemon juice

1 tbsp orange juice

1 tbsp demerara sugar

25 g/1 oz blanched almonds,
   chopped

2 tbsp apricot jam

1 Grease and flour two 18-cm/
7-inch sandwich cake tins. Put the
chocolate, grenadine and syrup in the
top of a double boiler or in a heatproof
bowl set over a pan of barely simmering
water. Stir over a low heat until the
chocolate has melted and the mixture
is smooth. Remove the pan from the
heat and leave the mixture to cool.

2 Cream the butter and caster sugar
together until pale and fluffy.
Gradually beat in the eggs then the
cooled chocolate mixture.

3 Sift the flour into another bowl
and stir in the ground rice.
Carefully fold the flour mixture into
the creamed mixture.

4 Divide the mixture between
the prepared tins and smooth
the surface. Bake in a preheated oven,
180°C/350°F/Gas Mark 4, for
20–25 minutes, until golden and firm
to the touch. Turn out on to a wire rack
and leave the cakes to cool.

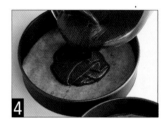

5 To make the filling, put all the
ingredients into a saucepan and
stir over a low heat for 4–5 minutes,
until fully incorporated. Remove from
the heat, leave to cool and then use
the filling to sandwich the cakes
together. Dust the top of the cake
with icing sugar to decorate.

white truffle cake

serves twelve

2 eggs

4 tbsp caster sugar

5½ tbsp plain flour

50 g/1¾ oz white chocolate, melted

TRUFFLE TOPPING

300 ml/10 fl oz double cream

350 g/12 oz white chocolate,
   broken into pieces

250 g/9 oz Quark or fromage frais

TO DECORATE

dark, milk or white chocolate
   caraque (see page 7)

cocoa powder, for dusting

1 Grease a 20-cm/8-inch round springform cake tin and line.

2 Whisk the eggs and caster sugar in a mixing bowl for 10 minutes or until very light and foamy and the whisk leaves a trail that lasts a few seconds when lifted. Sift the flour and fold in with a metal spoon. Fold in the melted white chocolate. Pour into the tin and bake in a preheated oven, 180°C/350°F/Gas Mark 4, for 25 minutes or until springy to the touch. Leave to cool slightly, then transfer to a wire rack until completely cold. Return the cold cake to the tin.

3 To make the topping, place the cream in a saucepan and bring to the boil, stirring to prevent it sticking to the base of the pan. Cool slightly,

then add the white chocolate pieces and stir until melted and combined. Remove from the heat and leave until almost cool, stirring, then stir in the Quark or fromage frais. Pour the mixture on top of the cake and chill for 2 hours.

4 Remove the cake from the tin and transfer to a serving plate. Make the caraque and then use it to decorate the top of the cake. Dust with cocoa powder and serve.

chocolate & vanilla loaf

serves ten

175 g/6 oz caster sugar

175 g/6 oz soft margarine

½ tsp vanilla essence

3 eggs

225 g/8 oz self-raising flour, sifted

50 g/1¾ oz plain chocolate

icing sugar, for dusting

COOK'S TIP

Freeze the cake undecorated
for up to 2 months. Thaw
at room temperature.

1 Lightly grease a 450-g/1-lb
loaf tin and set aside.

2 Using a wooden spoon, beat the
sugar and margarine together in a
bowl until light and fluffy.

3 Beat in the vanilla essence, then
gradually add the eggs, beating
well after each addition. Carefully fold
in the flour.

4 Divide the mixture in half. Gently
melt the plain chocolate and stir it
carefully into one half of the mixture
until well combined.

5 Place the vanilla mixture in the
tin and smooth the top. Spread
the chocolate over the vanilla layer.

6 Bake in a preheated oven, 190°C/
375°F/Gas Mark 5, for 30 minutes
or until springy to the touch.

7 Leave to cool in the tin for a few
minutes before transferring to a
wire rack to cool completely.

8 Serve the chocolate and vanilla
loaf dusted with icing sugar.

no-bake refrigerator cake

serves eight

225 g/8 oz unsalted butter, diced

225 g/8 oz plain chocolate, broken
into pieces

55 g/2 oz glacé cherries, chopped

55 g/2 oz walnuts, chopped

12 rectangular plain chocolate
biscuits

1 Line a 450-g/1-lb loaf tin with greaseproof paper or baking paper. Set aside.

2 Put the butter and chocolate into the top of a double boiler, or in a heatproof bowl set over a saucepan of barely simmering water. Stir constantly over a low heat until they have melted and the mixture is smooth. Remove from the heat and leave to cool slightly.

3 Mix the cherries and walnuts together in a separate bowl. Spoon one-third of the chocolate mixture into the prepared tin, cover with a layer of biscuits and top with half the cherries and walnuts. Make further layers, ending with the chocolate mixture. Cover with clingfilm and chill for at least 12 hours. When thoroughly chilled, turn the cake out on to a serving dish.

chocolate ganache cake

serves ten

175 g/6 oz butter

175 g/6 oz caster sugar

4 eggs, beaten lightly

200 g/7 oz self-raising flour

1 tbsp cocoa powder

50 g/1¾ oz plain chocolate, melted

GANACHE

450 ml/16 fl oz double cream

375 g/13 oz plain chocolate, broken
into pieces

200 g/7 oz chocolate-flavoured
cake covering, to finish

1 Lightly grease a 20-cm/8-inch springform cake tin and line the base. Beat the butter and sugar until light and fluffy. Gradually add the eggs, beating well. Sift together the flour and cocoa powder. Fold into the cake mixture. Fold in the melted chocolate.

2 Pour into the prepared tin and smooth the top. Bake in a preheated oven, 180°C/350°F/Gas Mark 4, for 40 minutes or until springy to the touch. Leave for 5 minutes, then turn out on to a wire rack and cool completely. When cold cut the cake into 2 layers.

3 To make the ganache, place the cream in a pan and bring to the boil, stirring. Add the chocolate and stir until melted and combined. Pour into a bowl and whisk for about 5 minutes or until the ganache is fluffy.

4 Reserve one-third of the ganache. Use the remaining ganache to sandwich the cake together and to spread smoothly and evenly over the top and sides of the cake.

5 Melt the chocolate-flavoured cake covering and spread it over a large sheet of baking paper. Cool until just set. Cut into strips a little wider than the height of the cake. Place the strips around the sides of the cake, overlapping them slightly.

6 Pipe the reserved ganache in tear drops or shells to cover the top of the cake. Leave the finished cake to chill for 1 hour in the refrigerator before serving.

chocolate truffle cake

serves twelve

75 g/2¾ oz butter

75 g/2¾ oz caster sugar

2 eggs, beaten lightly

75 g/2¾ oz self-raising flour

½ tsp baking powder

25 g/1 oz cocoa powder

50 g/1¾ oz ground almonds

TRUFFLE TOPPING

350 g/12 oz plain chocolate

100 g/3½ oz butter

300 ml/10 fl oz double cream

75 g/2¾ oz plain cake crumbs

3 tbsp dark rum

TO DECORATE

Cape gooseberries

50 g/1¾ oz plain chocolate, melted

1 Lightly grease a 20-cm/8-inch round springform cake tin and line the base. Set aside. Beat the butter and sugar together until light and fluffy. Gradually add the eggs to the creamed butter and sugar, beating well after each addition.

2 Sift the flour, baking powder and cocoa powder together and fold into the mixture along with the ground almonds. Pour into the prepared tin and bake in a preheated oven, 180°C/350°F/Gas Mark 4, for 20–25 minutes or until springy to the touch. Leave to cool slightly in the tin, then transfer to a wire rack to cool completely. Wash and dry the tin and return the cooled cake to the tin.

3 To make the topping, heat the chocolate, butter and cream in a heavy-based saucepan over a low heat and stir until smooth. Cool, then chill for 30 minutes. Beat well with a wooden spoon and chill for a further 30 minutes. Beat the mixture again, then add the cake crumbs and rum, beating until well combined. Spoon over the sponge base and leave to chill in the refrigerator for 3 hours.

4 Meanwhile, dip the Cape gooseberries in the melted chocolate until partially covered. Leave to set on baking paper. Transfer the chocolate truffle cake to a serving plate, decorate with the chocolate-dipped Cape gooseberries and serve.

bûche de noël

serves ten

CAKE

4 eggs

100 g/3½ oz caster sugar

75 g/2¾ oz self-raising flour

2 tbsp cocoa powder

ICING

150 g/5½ oz plain chocolate

2 egg yolks

150 ml/5 fl oz milk

125 g/4½ oz butter

4 tbsp icing sugar

2 tbsp rum, optional

TO DECORATE

a little white glacé or royal icing

icing sugar, for dusting

holly or Christmas cake decorations

1 Grease and line a 30 x 23-cm/ 12 x 9-inch Swiss roll tin.

2 Whisk the eggs and caster sugar in a bowl with an electric mixer for 10 minutes or until the mixture is light and foamy and the whisk leaves a trail. Sift the flour and cocoa powder and fold in. Pour into the tin and bake in a preheated oven, 200°C/400°F/Gas Mark 6, for 12 minutes or until springy to the touch. Turn out on to baking paper sprinkled with caster sugar. Peel off the lining paper and trim the edges. Cut a small slit halfway into the cake, about 1 cm/½ inch from one short end. Starting at that end, roll up, enclosing the paper. Leave the sponge to cool on a wire rack.

3 To make the icing, break the chocolate into pieces and melt over a saucepan of hot water. Beat in the egg yolks, whisk in the milk and cook, stirring until the mixture thickens enough to coat the back of a wooden spoon. Cover with dampened greaseproof paper and cool. Beat the butter and sugar until pale and fluffy. Beat in the custard and rum (if using).

4 Unroll the sponge, spread with one-third of the icing and roll up again. Place on a serving plate. Spread the remaining icing over the cake and mark with a fork to give the effect of tree bark. Leave to set. Pipe white icing at the ends to form the rings of the log. Sprinkle with sugar and decorate.

chocolate bread pudding

serves four

6 thick slices white bread, crusts
   removed

450 ml/16 fl oz milk

175 ml/6 fl oz canned evaporated
   milk

2 tbsp cocoa powder

2 eggs

2 tbsp dark muscovado sugar

1 tsp vanilla essence

icing sugar, for dusting

HOT FUDGE SAUCE

55 g/2 oz plain chocolate, broken
   into pieces

1 tbsp cocoa powder

2 tbsp golden syrup

5 g/2 oz butter or margarine

2 tbsp dark muscovado sugar

150 ml/5 fl oz milk

1 tbsp cornflour

1 Grease a shallow ovenproof dish. Cut the bread into squares and layer them in the dish.

2 Put the milk, evaporated milk and cocoa powder in a saucepan and heat gently, stirring occasionally, until the mixture is lukewarm.

3 Whisk the eggs, sugar and vanilla essence together. Add the warm milk mixture and beat well.

4 Pour into the prepared dish, making sure that all the bread is completely covered. Cover the dish with clingfilm and chill in the refrigerator for 1–2 hours.

5 Bake the pudding in a preheated oven, 180°C/350°F/Gas Mark 4, for about 35–40 minutes, until set. Remove the pudding from the oven and leave to stand for 5 minutes.

6 To make the sauce, put the chocolate, cocoa powder, syrup, butter or margarine, sugar, milk and cornflour into a saucepan. Heat gently, stirring constantly, until smooth.

7 Dust the pudding with icing sugar and serve at once with the hot fudge sauce.

chocolate layer log

serves eight

125 g/4½ oz soft margarine

125 g/4½ oz caster sugar

2 eggs

100 g/3½ oz self-raising flour

25 g/1 oz cocoa powder

2 tbsp milk

WHITE CHOCOLATE BUTTER CREAM

75 g/2¾ oz white chocolate

2 tbsp milk

150 g/5½ oz butter

125 g/4½ oz icing sugar

2 tbsp orange-flavoured liqueur

quick chocolate curls (see page 7),
   to decorate

1 Grease and line the sides of two
400-g/14-oz food cans.

2 Beat the margarine and sugar
together in a bowl until light and
fluffy. Gradually add the eggs, beating
well after each addition. Sift the flour
and cocoa powder together and fold
into the cake mixture. Fold in the milk.

3 Divide the mixture between the 2
prepared cans. Stand the cans on
a baking tray and bake in a preheated
oven, 180°C/350°F/Gas Mark 4, for 40
minutes or until springy to the touch.
Leave to cool for about 5 minutes in
the cans, then turn out and leave to
cool completely on a wire rack.

4 To make the butter cream, heat
the chocolate and milk gently in
a pan until the chocolate has melted,
stirring until combined. Leave to cool
slightly. Beat together the butter and
icing sugar until light and fluffy. Beat
in the orange liqueur. Gradually beat
in the chocolate mixture.

5 Cut both cakes into 1-cm/½-inch
thick slices, then reassemble them
by sandwiching the slices together
with some of the butter cream.

6 Place the cake on a serving plate
and spread the remaining butter
cream over the top and sides. Decorate
with chocolate curls, then serve cut
diagonally into slices.

chocolate & apricot squares

serves twelve

125 g/4½ oz butter

175 g/6 oz white chocolate,

   chopped

4 eggs

125 g/4½ oz caster sugar

200 g/7 oz plain flour, sifted

1 tsp baking powder

pinch of salt

100 g/3½ oz no-soak dried apricots,

   chopped

1 Lightly grease a 20-cm/8-inch square cake tin and line the base with a sheet of baking paper.

2 Melt the butter and chocolate in a heatproof bowl set over a saucepan of simmering water. Stir frequently with a wooden spoon until the mixture is smooth and glossy. Leave the mixture to cool slightly.

3 Beat the eggs and caster sugar into the butter and chocolate mixture until well combined.

4 Fold in the flour, baking powder, salt and chopped dried apricots and mix together well so all the ingredients are combined.

5 Pour the mixture into the prepared tin and bake in a preheated oven, 180°C/350°F/Gas Mark 4, for about 25–30 minutes.

6 The centre of the cake may not be completely firm, but it will set as it cools. Leave in the tin to cool.

7 When the cake is completely cold turn it out and slice into squares or bars to serve.

Hot Desserts

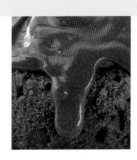

Chocolate is comforting at any time but no more so than when served in a steaming hot pudding. It is hard to think of anything more warming, comforting and homely than tucking into a steamed hot Chocolate Fudge Pudding or a Hot Chocolate Soufflé, and children will love the chocolate addition to nursery favourites such as the chocolate Bread & Butter Pudding. In fact, there are several old favourites that have been given the chocolate treatment, bringing them bang up to date and putting them on the chocolate lover's map.

When you are feeling in need of something a little more sophisticated, try the new-style Chocolate Apple Pancake Stacks, or Chocolate Pear & Almond Flan, or Chocolate Zabaglione for an elegant creamy, warm dessert set to get your taste buds in a whirl!

chocolate ginger puddings

serves four

100 g/3½ oz soft margarine

100 g/3½ oz self-raising flour, sifted

100 g/3½ oz caster sugar

2 eggs

25 g/1 oz cocoa powder, sifted

25 g/1 oz plain chocolate

50 g/1¾ oz stem ginger

CHOCOLATE CUSTARD

2 egg yolks

1 tbsp caster sugar

1 tbsp cornflour

300 ml/10 fl oz milk

100 g/3½ oz plain chocolate,
    broken into pieces

icing sugar, for dusting

1 Lightly grease 4 individual pudding basins. Place the margarine, flour, sugar, eggs and cocoa powder in a mixing bowl and beat until well combined and smooth. Chop the chocolate and ginger and stir into the mixture, ensuring they are well combined.

2 Spoon the cake mixture into the prepared basins and smooth the top. The mixture should three-quarters fill the basins. Cover the basins with discs of baking paper and cover with a pleated sheet of foil. Steam the chocolate ginger puddings for 45 minutes, until the puddings are cooked and springy to the touch.

3 Meanwhile, make the chocolate custard. Beat together the egg yolks, sugar and cornflour to form a smooth paste. Heat the milk until boiling and pour over the egg mixture. Return to the pan and cook over a very low heat, stirring until thick. Remove the pan from the heat and beat in the chocolate. Stir gently until the chocolate melts.

4 Lift the puddings from the steamer, run a knife around the edge of the basins and carefully turn out on to serving plates. Dust each pudding with sugar and drizzle some chocolate custard over the top. Serve the remaining chocolate custard separately.

chocolate queen of puddings

serves four

50 g/1¾ oz plain chocolate

450 ml/16 fl oz chocolate-flavoured
    milk

100 g/3½ oz fresh white or
    wholemeal breadcrumbs

125 g/4½ oz caster sugar

2 eggs, separated

4 tbsp black cherry jam

VARIATION

If you prefer, add 40 g/1½ oz
desiccated coconut to the
breadcrumbs and omit the jam.

1 Break the chocolate into small
pieces and place in a saucepan
with the chocolate-flavoured milk. Heat
gently, stirring until the chocolate
melts. Bring almost to the boil, then
remove the pan from the heat.

2 Place the breadcrumbs in a large
mixing bowl with 25 g/1 oz of the
sugar. Pour over the chocolate milk and
mix well. Beat in the egg yolks.

3 Spoon into a 1.2-litre/2-pint pie
dish and bake in a preheated
oven, 180°C/350°F/Gas Mark 4, for
25–30 minutes or until the pudding is
set and firm to the touch.

4 Whisk the egg whites in a large
clean bowl until standing
in soft peaks. Gradually whisk in the
remaining caster sugar and whisk until
you have a glossy, thick meringue.

5 Spread the jam over the chocolate
mixture and pile the meringue on
top. Return to the oven for about
15 minutes or until the meringue is
crisp and golden.

chocolate eve's pudding

serves four

2 eating apples, peeled, cored and
   sliced thickly
225 g/8 oz fresh or frozen
   raspberries
4 tbsp seedless raspberry jam
2 tbsp ruby port, optional
SPONGE TOPPING
4 tbsp soft margarine
4 tbsp caster sugar
75 g/2¾ oz self-raising flour, sifted
50 g/1¾ oz white chocolate, grated
1 egg
2 tbsp milk
BITTER CHOCOLATE SAUCE
85 g/3 oz plain chocolate
150 ml/5 fl oz single cream

VARIATION

Try using plain chocolate in the
sponge, and top with apricot
halves, covered with peach
schnapps and apricot jam.

1 Place the apple slices and
raspberries in a shallow
1.2-litre/2-pint ovenproof dish and
set aside while you warm the jam
and port if using.

2 Place the raspberry jam and port
in a small saucepan and heat
gently until the jam melts and combines
with the port. Pour the raspberry
mixture over the fruit.

3 Place all of the ingredients for the
sponge topping in a large mixing
bowl and beat thoroughly with an
electric mixer until the mixture is
completely smooth.

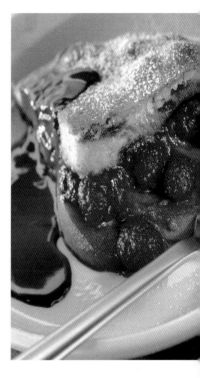

4 Spoon the sponge mixture over
the fruit and smooth the top.
Bake in a preheated oven,
180°C/350°F/Gas Mark 4, for 40–45
minutes or until the sponge is springy
to the touch.

5 To make the sauce, break the
chocolate into small pieces and
place in a heavy-based saucepan with
the cream. Heat gently, beating until a
smooth sauce is formed. Serve the
sauce warm with the pudding.

67

bread & butter pudding

serves four

225 g/8 oz brioche

15 g/½ oz butter

50 g/1¾ oz plain chocolate chips

1 egg

2 egg yolks

4 tbsp caster sugar

425 ml/15 fl oz canned evaporated
  milk

1 Cut the brioche into thin slices
using a sharp knife. Lightly butter
one side of each brioche slice.

2 Place a layer of brioche, buttered-
side down, in the bottom of a
shallow ovenproof dish. Sprinkle a few
chocolate chips over the top.

3 Continue layering the brioche and
chocolate chips, finishing with a
layer of bread on top.

VARIATION

For a double-chocolate
pudding, heat the milk with
1 tablespoon of cocoa powder,
stirring until well dissolved.
Continue from step 4.

4 Whisk the egg, egg yolks and
sugar together until combined.
Heat the milk in a small saucepan until
it just begins to simmer. Gradually add
to the egg mixture, whisking well.

5 Pour the custard over the pudding
and leave to stand for 5 minutes.
Press the brioche down into the milk.

6 Place the pudding in a roasting
tin and fill with boiling water to
come halfway up the side of the dish
(this is known as a bain-marie). Bake in
a preheated oven, 180°C/350°F/Gas
Mark 4, for 30 minutes or until the
custard has set. Leave the pudding
to cool for 5 minutes before serving.

chocolate fruit crumble

serves four

400 g/14 oz canned apricots in
    fruit juice
450 g/1 lb cooking apples, peeled
    and sliced thickly
100 g/3½ oz plain flour
85 g/3 oz butter
50 g/1¾ oz porridge oats
4 tbsp caster sugar
100 g/3½ oz chocolate chips

VARIATION

Other fruits can be used to make
this crumble – fresh pears mixed
with fresh or frozen raspberries
work well. If you do not use
canned fruit, add 4 tablespoons
of orange juice to the fresh fruit.

1 Lightly grease an ovenproof dish
with a little butter.

2 Drain the apricots, reserving
4 tablespoons of the juice. Place
the apples and apricots in the prepared
ovenproof dish with the reserved
apricot juice and toss to mix.

3 Sift the flour into a mixing bowl.
Cut the butter into small cubes
and rub in with your fingertips until the
mixture resembles fine breadcrumbs.
Stir in the porridge oats, caster sugar
and chocolate chips.

4 Sprinkle the crumble mixture
over the apples and apricots and
smooth the top roughly. Do not press
the crumble down on to the fruit.

5 Bake in a preheated oven,
180°C/350°F/Gas Mark 4, for
40–45 minutes or until the topping is
golden. Serve the crumble hot or cold.

69

chocolate & banana pancakes

serves four

3 large bananas

6 tbsp orange juice

grated rind of 1 orange

2 tbsp orange- or banana-flavoured
  liqueur

HOT CHOCOLATE SAUCE

1 tbsp cocoa powder

2 tsp cornflour

3 tbsp milk

40 g/1½ oz plain chocolate

15 g/½ oz butter

175 g/6 oz golden syrup

¼ tsp vanilla essence

PANCAKES

100 g/3½ oz plain flour

1 tbsp cocoa powder

1 egg

1 tsp sunflower oil

300 ml/10 fl oz milk

oil, for frying

1 Peel and slice the bananas and place them in a dish with the orange juice and rind and the liqueur. Set the bananas aside.

2 Mix the cocoa powder and cornflour in a bowl, then stir in the milk. Break the plain chocolate into pieces and place in a saucepan with the butter and golden syrup. Heat gently, stirring until well blended. Add the cocoa mixture and bring to the boil over a gentle heat, stirring. Simmer for 1 minute, then remove from the heat and stir in the vanilla essence.

3 To make the pancakes, sift the flour and cocoa into a mixing bowl and make a well in the centre. Add the egg and oil. Gradually whisk in the milk to form a smooth batter. Heat a little oil in a heavy-based frying pan and pour off any excess. Pour in a little batter and tilt the pan to coat the base. Cook over a medium heat until the underside is browned. Flip over and cook the other side. Slide the pancake out of the pan and keep warm. Repeat until all the pancake batter has been used up. Keep warm.

4 To serve, re-heat the chocolate sauce for 1–2 minutes. Fill the pancakes with the bananas and fold in half or into triangles. Pour a little chocolate sauce over the pancakes and serve immediately.

poached pears in chocolate

serves six

6 firm ripe pears

100 g/3½ oz caster sugar

2 cinnamon sticks

rind of 1 orange

2 cloves

1 bottle rosé wine

CHOCOLATE SAUCE

175 g/6 oz plain chocolate

250 g/9 oz mascarpone cheese

2 tbsp orange-flavoured liqueur

COOK'S TIP

There is no need to waste the poaching liquid. Boil it rapidly in a clean saucepan for 10 minutes to reduce to a syrup. Use to sweeten fresh fruit salad or spoon it over ice cream.

1 Carefully peel the pears, leaving the stalks intact.

2 Place the sugar, cinnamon sticks, orange rind, cloves and wine in a saucepan that will hold the pears.

3 Heat gently until the sugar has dissolved, then add the pears and bring to a simmer. Cover the pan and poach the pears gently for 20 minutes. If serving them cold, leave the pears to cool in the liquid and chill until required. If serving hot, leave the pears in the hot liquid whilst preparing the sauce.

4 To make the sauce, melt the chocolate. Beat together the mascarpone cheese and the liqueur. Beat the cheese mixture into the melted chocolate.

5 Remove the pears from the poaching liquid and place on a serving plate. Add a spoonful of sauce on the side and serve the remainder separately. Alternatively, pipe a rosette of the sauce on each plate.

chocolate pear & almond flan

serves six

100 g/3½ oz plain flour

25 g/1 oz ground almonds

70 g/2½ oz block margarine

about 3 tbsp water

FILLING

400 g/14 oz canned pear halves in
   fruit juice

55 g/2 oz butter

4 tbsp caster sugar

2 eggs, beaten

100 g/3½ oz ground almonds

2 tbsp cocoa powder

few drops of almond essence

icing sugar, for dusting

CHOCOLATE SAUCE

4 tbsp caster sugar

3 tbsp golden syrup

90 ml/3¼ fl oz water

175 g/6 oz plain chocolate, broken
   into pieces

25 g/1 oz butter

1 Grease a 20-cm/8-inch flan tin. Sift the flour into a mixing bowl and stir in the almonds. Rub in the margarine with your fingertips until the mixture resembles breadcrumbs. Add enough water to mix to a soft dough. Cover, chill in the freezer for 10 minutes, then roll out and use to line the tin. Prick the base and chill again.

2 Meanwhile, make the filling. Drain the pears well. Beat the butter and sugar until light and fluffy. Beat in the eggs. Fold in the almonds, cocoa powder and almond essence. Spread the chocolate mixture in the pastry case and arrange the pears on top, pressing down lightly. Bake in the centre of a preheated oven, 200°C/400°F/Gas Mark 6, for 30 minutes or until the filling has risen. Cool slightly and transfer to a serving dish, if liked. Dust with sugar.

3 To make the chocolate sauce, place the sugar, syrup and water in a saucepan and heat gently, stirring until the sugar dissolves. Boil gently for 1 minute. Remove from the heat, add the chocolate and butter and stir until melted and well combined. Serve the sauce with the flan.

chocolate apple pie

serves six

CHOCOLATE PASTRY

4 tbsp cocoa powder

200 g/7 oz plain flour

100 g/3½ oz softened butter

4 tbsp caster sugar

2 egg yolks

a few drops of vanilla essence

cold water, for mixing

FILLING

750 g/1 lb 10 oz cooking apples

25 g/1 oz butter

½ tsp ground cinnamon

50 g/1¾ oz plain chocolate chips

a little egg white, beaten

½ tsp caster sugar

whipped cream or vanilla ice cream,
    to serve (optional)

1 To make the pastry, sift the cocoa powder and flour into a mixing bowl and rub in the butter until the mixture resembles fine breadcrumbs. Stir in the caster sugar. Add the egg yolks, vanilla essence and enough water to mix to a dough.

2 Roll out the dough on a lightly floured work surface and use to line a deep 20-cm/8-inch cake tin. Chill for 30 minutes. Roll out any trimmings and cut out some pastry leaves to decorate the top of the pie.

3 Peel, core and thickly slice the apples. Place half of the apple slices in a saucepan with the butter and cinnamon and cook over a gentle heat, stirring occasionally until the apples have softened.

4 Stir in the uncooked apple slices, leave to cool slightly, then stir in the chocolate chips. Prick the base of the pastry case and pile the apple mixture into it. Arrange the pastry leaves on top. Brush the leaves with a little egg white and sprinkle with caster sugar.

5 Bake in a preheated oven, 180°C/350°F/Gas Mark 4, for 35 minutes, until the pastry is crisp. Serve the chocolate apple pie warm or cold, with a spoonful of whipped cream or vanilla ice cream.

chocolate fudge pudding

serves six

150 g/5½ oz soft margarine

150 g/5½ oz self-raising flour

150 g/5½ oz golden syrup

3 eggs

25 g/1 oz cocoa powder

CHOCOLATE FUDGE SAUCE

100 g/3½ oz plain chocolate

125 ml/4 fl oz condensed milk

4 tbsp double cream

1 Lightly grease a 1.2-litre/2-pint pudding basin.

2 Place the ingredients for the sponge in a mixing bowl and beat until well combined and smooth.

3 Spoon into the prepared basin and smooth the top. Cover with a disc of baking paper and tie a pleated sheet of foil over the basin. Steam for 1½–2 hours, until the pudding is cooked and springy to the touch.

4 To make the sauce, break the chocolate into small pieces and place in a small saucepan with the condensed milk. Heat gently, stirring until the chocolate melts.

5 Remove the saucepan from the heat and stir in the cream.

6 To serve the pudding, turn it out on to a serving plate and pour over a little of the chocolate fudge sauce. Serve the remaining sauce separately.

chocolate meringue pie

serves six

225 g/8 oz plain chocolate digestive
  biscuits

55 g/2 oz butter

FILLING

3 egg yolks

4 tbsp caster sugar

4 tbsp cornflour

600 ml/1 pint milk

100 g/3½ oz plain chocolate,
  melted

MERINGUE

2 egg whites

100 g/3½ oz caster sugar

¼ tsp vanilla essence

1 Place the digestive biscuits in a polythene bag and crush with a rolling pin. Pour into a mixing bowl. Melt the butter and stir it into the biscuit crumbs until well mixed. Press the biscuit mixture firmly into the base and up the sides of a 23-cm/9-inch flan tin or dish.

2 To make the filling, beat the egg yolks, caster sugar and cornflour in a large bowl until they form a smooth paste, adding a little of the milk if necessary. Heat the milk until almost boiling, then slowly pour it on to the egg mixture, whisking well.

3 Return the mixture to the saucepan and cook gently, whisking constantly, until it thickens. Remove from the heat. Whisk in the melted chocolate, then pour it on to the digestive biscuit base.

4 To make the meringue, whisk the egg whites in a large mixing bowl until standing in soft peaks. Gradually whisk in about two-thirds of the sugar until the mixture is stiff and glossy. Fold the remaining sugar and vanilla essence into the meringue.

5 Spread the meringue over the filling, swirling the surface with the back of a spoon to give it an attractive finish. Bake in the centre of a preheated oven, 160°C/325°F/Gas Mark 3, for 30 minutes or until golden. Serve hot or just warm.

apple pancake stacks

serves four

225 g/8 oz plain flour

1½ tsp baking powder

4 tbsp caster sugar

1 egg

15 g/½ oz butter, melted

300 ml10 fl oz milk

1 eating apple

50 g/1¾ oz plain chocolate chips

Chocolate Sauce (see page 82) or

    maple syrup, to serve

COOK'S TIP

To keep the cooked pancakes
warm, pile them on top of each
other with baking paper in
between to prevent them
sticking to one another.

1 Sift the flour and baking powder into a mixing bowl. Stir in the caster sugar. Make a well in the centre and add the egg and melted butter. Gradually whisk in the milk to form a smooth batter.

2 Peel, core and grate the apple and stir it into the batter together with the chocolate chips.

3 Heat a griddle or heavy-based frying pan over a medium heat and grease it lightly. For each pancake, place about 2 tablespoons of the batter on to the griddle or frying pan and spread to make a 7.5-cm/3-inch round.

4 Cook for a few minutes until you see bubbles appear on the surface of the pancake. Turn over and cook for a further 1 minute. Remove from the pan and keep warm. Repeat with the remaining batter to make about 12 pancakes.

5 To serve, stack 3 or 4 pancakes on an individual serving plate and serve them with the Chocolate Sauce or maple syrup.

chocolate fondue

serves four

CHOCOLATE FONDUE

225 g/8 oz plain chocolate

200 ml/7 fl oz double cream

2 tbsp brandy

TO SERVE

selection of fruit

white and pink marshmallows

sweet biscuits

1 Break the chocolate into small pieces and place in a small saucepan with the cream.

2 Heat the mixture gently, stirring constantly, until the chocolate has melted and blended with the cream.

COOK'S TIP

To prepare the fruit for dipping, cut larger fruit into bite-sized pieces. Fruit that discolours, such as bananas, apples and pears, should be dipped in a little lemon juice as soon as it is cut.

3 Remove the pan from the heat and stir in the brandy.

4 Pour into a fondue pot or a small flameproof dish and keep warm, preferably over a small burner.

5 Serve with a selection of fruit, marshmallows and biscuits for dipping. The fruit and marshmallows can be spiked on fondue forks, wooden skewers or ordinary forks.

chocolate ravioli

serves four

175 g/6 oz plain flour

4 tbsp cocoa powder

2 tbsp icing sugar

2 eggs, beaten lightly, plus 1 extra
egg, beaten, for brushing.

1 tbsp vegetable oil

FILLING

175 g/6 oz white chocolate, broken
into pieces

225 g/8 oz mascarpone cheese

1 egg

1 tbsp finely chopped stem ginger

fresh mint sprigs, to decorate

double cream, to serve

1 Sift the flour, cocoa powder and sugar together on to a clean work surface. Make a well in the centre and pour the 2 beaten eggs and the oil into it. Gradually draw in the flour with your fingertips until it is fully incorporated. Alternatively, sift the flour, cocoa and sugar into a food processor, add the eggs and oil and process until mixed. Knead the dough until it is smooth and elastic, then cover with clingfilm and place in the refrigerator for 30 minutes to chill.

2 Meanwhile, to make the filling, put the white chocolate into the top of a double boiler or in a heatproof bowl set over a saucepan of barely simmering water. When the chocolate has melted, remove it from the heat and cool slightly, then beat in the mascarpone cheese and the egg. Stir in the chopped stem ginger.

3 Remove the pasta dough from the refrigerator, cut it in half and keep one half tightly wrapped in clingfilm. Roll out the first half of the dough into a rectangle on a lightly floured work surface, then cover with a clean, damp tea towel. Roll out the other half into a rectangle. Spoon the chocolate and ginger filling into a piping bag and pipe small mounds in even rows at intervals of about 4 cm/1½ inches over 1 dough rectangle. Brush the spaces between the mounds with beaten egg, then, using a rolling pin to lift it,

position the second dough rectangle on top of the first. Press firmly between the mounds with your finger to seal and push out any pockets of air. Cut the dough into squares around the mounds using a serrated ravioli or pastry cutter or a sharp knife. Transfer the ravioli to a lightly floured tea towel and leave to rest for 30 minutes.

4 Bring a large saucepan of water to the boil, then lower the heat to medium and cook the ravioli, in batches, stirring to prevent them from sticking together, for 4–5 minutes, until tender, but still firm to the bite. Remove with a slotted spoon. Serve immediately on individual plates, garnished with mint sprigs and handing the cream separately.

saucy chocolate pudding

serves four

300 ml/10 fl oz milk

75 g/2¾ oz plain chocolate

½ tsp vanilla essence

100 g/3½ oz caster sugar

100 g/3½ oz butter

150 g/5½ oz self-raising flour

2 tbsp cocoa powder

icing sugar, for dusting

CHOCOLATE SAUCE

3 tbsp cocoa powder

4 tbsp light muscovado sugar

300 ml/10 fl oz boiling water

1 Lightly grease a 850-ml/1½-pint ovenproof dish.

2 Place the milk in a small saucepan. Break the chocolate into pieces and add to the milk. Heat gently, stirring until the chocolate melts. Cool slightly. Stir in the vanilla essence.

3 Beat the caster sugar and butter together in a bowl until light and fluffy. Sift the flour and cocoa powder together. Add to the bowl with the chocolate milk and beat until smooth. Pour the mixture into the prepared dish.

4 To make the sauce, mix the cocoa powder and sugar together in a bowl. Add a little boiling water to the mixture and stir to a smooth paste, then stir in the remaining water. Pour the chocolate sauce over the surface of the pudding but do not mix in.

5 Place the dish on a baking tray and bake in a preheated oven, 180°C/350°F/Gas Mark 4, for 40 minutes or until the pudding is dry on top and springy to the touch. Leave the pudding to stand for about 5 minutes, then dust lightly with a little icing sugar just before serving.

pecan & fudge ring

serves six

FUDGE SAUCE

40 g/1½ oz butter

3 tbsp light muscovado sugar

4 tbsp golden syrup

2 tbsp milk

1 tbsp cocoa powder

40 g/1½ oz plain chocolate

50 g/1¾ oz pecan nuts, chopped
finely

CAKE

100 g/3½ oz soft margarine

100 g/3½ oz light muscovado sugar

125 g/4½ oz self-raising flour

2 eggs

2 tbsp milk

1 tbsp golden syrup

1 Lightly grease a 20-cm/8-inch
ring tin with a little butter.

2 To make the fudge sauce, place
the butter, sugar, syrup, milk and
cocoa powder in a small saucepan and
heat gently, stirring until combined.

3 Break the chocolate into pieces,
add to the mixture and stir until
melted. Stir in the chopped nuts. Pour
into the base of the tin and cool.

4 To make the cake, place all of the
ingredients in a mixing bowl and
beat until smooth. Carefully spoon the
cake mixture over the chocolate fudge
sauce in the base of the tin.

5 Bake in a preheated oven,
180°C/350°F/Gas Mark 4, for
35 minutes or until the cake is springy
to the touch.

6 Leave to cool in the tin for
5 minutes, then turn out on
to a serving plate.

hot chocolate soufflé

serves four

100 g/3½ oz plain chocolate
300 ml/10 fl oz milk
25 g/1 oz butter
4 large eggs, separated
1 tbsp cornflour
4 tbsp caster sugar
½ tsp vanilla essence
100 g/3½ oz plain chocolate chips
caster and icing sugar, for dusting
CHOCOLATE CUSTARD
2 tbsp cornflour
1 tbsp caster sugar
450 ml/16 fl oz milk
50 g/1¾ oz plain chocolate

1 Grease a 850-ml/1½-pint soufflé dish and sprinkle with caster sugar. Break the chocolate into pieces.

2 Heat the milk with the butter in a saucepan until almost boiling. Mix the egg yolks, cornflour and caster sugar in a bowl and pour on some of the hot milk, whisking. Return it to the pan and cook gently, stirring constantly until thickened. Add the chocolate and stir until melted. Remove from the heat and stir in the vanilla essence.

3 Whisk the egg whites until standing in soft peaks. Fold half of the egg whites into the chocolate mixture. Fold in the rest with the chocolate chips. Pour into the dish

and bake in a preheated oven, 180°C/350°F/Gas Mark 4, for 40–45 minutes, until well risen.

4 Meanwhile, make the custard. Put the cornflour and sugar in a small bowl and mix to a smooth paste with a little of the milk. Heat the remaining milk until almost boiling. Pour a little of the hot milk on to the cornflour, mix well, then pour back into the saucepan. Cook gently, stirring until thickened. Break the chocolate into pieces and add to the custard, stirring until melted.

5 Dust the soufflé with sugar and serve immediately with the chocolate custard.

fudge pudding

serves four

55 g/2 oz margarine

6 tbsp soft light brown sugar

2 eggs, beaten

350 ml/12 fl oz milk

50 g/1¾ oz chopped walnuts

5 tbsp plain flour

2 tbsp cocoa powder

icing sugar and cocoa powder,
   for dusting

1 Lightly grease a 1-litre/1¾-pint ovenproof dish.

2 Cream the margarine and sugar together in a large mixing bowl until fluffy. Beat in the eggs.

3 Gradually stir in the milk, using a whisk, and add the walnuts.

4 Sift the flour and cocoa powder into the mixture and fold in gently, with a metal spoon, until well mixed and thoroughly combined.

5 Spoon the mixture into the dish and cook in a preheated oven, 180°C/350°F/Gas Mark 4, for 35–40 minutes or until the sponge is cooked.

6 Dust with icing sugar and cocoa powder and serve.

chocolate zabaglione

serves four

4 egg yolks

4 tbsp caster sugar

50 g/1¾ oz plain chocolate

125 ml/4 fl oz Marsala wine

cocoa powder, for dusting

COOK'S TIP

Make the dessert just before serving as it will separate if left to stand. If it begins to curdle, remove it from the heat immediately and place it in a bowl of cold water to stop the cooking. Whisk the chocolate zabaglione furiously until the mixture comes together.

1 Whisk together the egg yolks and caster sugar in a large mixing bowl with an electric mixer, until the mixture is very pale.

2 Grate the chocolate finely and fold into the egg yolk and caster sugar mixture.

3 Fold the Marsala wine into the chocolate mixture.

4 Place the mixing bowl over a saucepan of gently simmering water and set the electric mixer on the lowest speed or swap to a balloon whisk. Cook gently, whisking constantly until the mixture thickens. Take care not to overcook or the mixture will curdle. If this happens follow the Cook's Tip.

5 Spoon the hot mixture into warmed individual glass dishes or coffee cups (as here) and dust with cocoa powder. Serve the zabaglione as soon as possible, while it is still warm, light and fluffy.

steamed coffee sponge

serves four

25 g/1 oz margarine

2 tbsp soft brown sugar

2 eggs

5½ tbsp plain flour

¾ tsp baking powder

6 tbsp milk

1 tsp coffee essence

SAUCE

300 ml/10 fl oz milk

1 tbsp soft brown sugar

1 tsp cocoa powder

2 tbsp cornflour

1 Lightly grease a 600-ml/1-pint heatproof pudding basin. Cream the margarine and sugar until light and fluffy and beat in the eggs.

2 Gradually stir in the flour and baking powder and then the milk and coffee essence to make a smooth batter.

3 Spoon the mixture into the pudding basin and cover with a pleated piece of baking paper and then a pleated piece of foil, securing around the bowl with string. Place in a steamer or large saucepan half full of boiling water. Cover and steam for 1–1¼ hours or until cooked through.

4 To make the sauce, put the milk, soft brown sugar and cocoa powder in a pan and heat until the sugar dissolves. Blend the cornflour with 4 tablespoons of cold water to make a paste and stir into the saucepan. Bring the sauce to the boil, stirring constantly until thickened. Cook over a gentle heat for 1 minute.

5 Turn the pudding out on to a serving plate and spoon the sauce over the top. Serve.

COOK'S TIP

The pudding is covered with pleated paper and foil to allow it to rise. The foil will react with the steam and must therefore not be placed directly against the pudding.

chocolate pudding with rum

serves four

55 g/2 oz unsalted butter

175 g/6 oz self-raising flour

55 g/2 oz plain chocolate

¼ tsp vanilla essence

115 g/4 oz caster sugar

2 eggs, beaten lightly

5 tbsp milk

SAUCE

300 ml/10 fl oz milk

2 tbsp cornflour

2 tbsp caster sugar

2 tbsp dark rum

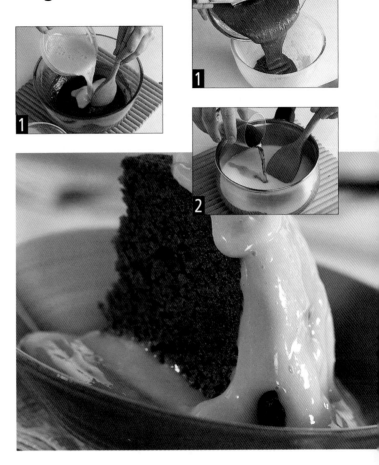

1 Grease and flour a 1.2-litre/ 2-pint pudding basin. Put the butter, chocolate and vanilla essence in the top of a double boiler or in a heatproof bowl set over a saucepan of simmering water. Heat gently until melted, then remove from the heat and cool slightly. Stir in the sugar, then beat in the eggs. Sift in the flour, stir in the milk, and mix well. Pour into the prepared pudding basin, cover the top with foil and tie with string. Steam the pudding for 1 hour, topping up with boiling water if necessary.

2 To make the sauce, pour the milk into a small saucepan set over a medium heat. Stir in the cornflour, then stir in the sugar until dissolved. Bring to the boil, stirring constantly, then lower the heat and simmer until thickened and smooth. Remove from the heat and stir in the rum.

3 To serve, remove the pudding from the heat and discard the foil. Run a round-bladed knife around the side of the basin, place a serving plate on top of the pudding and, holding them together, invert. Serve the pudding immediately, handing the rum sauce separately.

sticky chocolate puddings

serves six

125 g/4½ oz butter, softened

150 g/5½ oz soft brown sugar

3 eggs, beaten

pinch of salt

25 g/1 oz cocoa powder

125 g/4½ oz self-raising flour

25 g/1 oz plain chocolate, chopped
finely

75 g/2¾ oz white chocolate,
chopped finely

SAUCE

150 ml/5 fl oz double cream

75 g/2¾ oz soft brown sugar

25 g/1 oz butter

1 Lightly grease 6 individual 175-ml/6 fl-oz pudding basins.

2 Cream the butter and sugar together in a bowl until pale and fluffy. Beat in the eggs a little at a time, beating well after each addition.

3 Sift the salt, cocoa powder and flour into the creamed mixture and fold through the mixture. Stir in the chopped chocolate until evenly combined.

4 Divide the mixture between the prepared pudding basins. Lightly grease 6 squares of foil and use them to cover the tops of the basins. Press around the edges to seal.

5 Place the basins in a roasting tin and pour in boiling water to come halfway up the sides of the basins.

6 Bake in a preheated oven, 180°/350°F/ Gas Mark 4, for 50 minutes or until a skewer inserted into the centre comes out clean.

7 Remove the basins from the roasting tin and set aside while you prepare the sauce.

8 To make the sauce, put the cream, sugar and butter into a saucepan and bring to the boil over a gentle heat. Simmer gently until the sugar has competely dissolved.

9 To serve, run a knife around the edge of each pudding, then turn out on to serving plates. Pour the cream sauce over the top of the puddings and serve immediately.

tropical fruit kebabs

serves four

DIP

125 g/4½ oz plain chocolate,
   broken into pieces

2 tbsp golden syrup

1 tbsp cocoa powder

1 tbsp cornflour

200 ml/7 fl oz milk

KEBABS

1 mango

1 paw-paw

2 kiwi fruit

½ small pineapple

1 large banana

2 tbsp lemon juice

150 ml/5 fl oz white rum

1 Put all of the ingredients for the chocolate dip into a heavy-based saucepan. Heat over the barbecue or a low heat, stirring constantly, until thickened and smooth. Keep warm at the edge of the barbecue.

2 Slice the mango on each side of its large, flat stone. Cut the flesh into chunks, removing the peel. Halve, deseed and peel the paw-paw and cut it into chunks. Peel the kiwi fruit and slice into chunks. Peel the pineapple and cut it into chunks. Peel and slice the banana and dip the pieces in the lemon juice, turning them to coat evenly to prevent it from discolouring.

3 Thread the pieces of fruit alternately on to 4 wooden skewers. Place them in a shallow dish and pour over the rum. Leave to soak up the flavour of the rum for at least 30 minutes, until ready to barbecue.

4 Cook the kebabs over the hot coals, turning frequently, for about 2 minutes, until seared. Serve, accompanied by the hot chocolate dip.

stuffed nectarines

serves six

85 g/3 oz dark continental
    chocolate, chopped finely
55 g/2 oz amaretti biscuit crumbs
1 tsp finely grated lemon rind
1 large egg white
6 tbsp Amaretto liqueur
6 nectarines, halved and stoned
300 ml/10 fl oz white wine
55 g/2 oz milk chocolate, grated
whipped cream or vanilla or
    chocolate ice cream, to serve

1 Mix the chocolate, amaretti crumbs and lemon rind together in a bowl. Lightly beat the egg white and add it to the mixture with half the Amaretto liqueur. Using a small sharp knife, slightly enlarge the cavities in the nectarines. Add the removed nectarine flesh to the chocolate and crumb mixture and mix well.

2 Preheat the oven to 190°C/375°F/ Gas Mark 5. Place the nectarines, cut-side up, in an ovenproof dish just large enough to hold them in a single layer. Pile the chocolate and crumb mixture into the cavities, dividing it equally among them. Mix the wine and remaining Amaretto and pour it into the dish around the nectarines. Bake in

a preheated oven, for 40–45 minutes, until the nectarines are tender. Transfer 2 nectarine halves to each individual serving plate and spoon over a little of the cooking juices. Sprinkle over the grated milk chocolate and serve the nectarines immediately with whipped cream or, if you prefer, vanilla or chocolate ice cream.

banana empanadas

serves four

about 8 sheets of filo pastry, cut into
half lengthways

melted butter or vegetable oil, for
brushing

2 ripe sweet bananas

1–2 tsp sugar

juice of ½ lemon

175–200 g/6–7 oz plain chocolate,
broken into small pieces

icing sugar, for dusting

ground cinnamon, for dusting

COOK'S TIP

You could use ready-made puff
pastry instead of filo for a more
puffed-up effect.

1 Working one at a time, lay
a long rectangular sheet of filo
pastry out in front of you and brush it
all over with butter or oil.

2 Peel and dice the bananas and
place in a bowl. Add the sugar
and lemon juice and stir well to
combine. Stir in the chocolate.

3 Place 2 teaspoons of the banana
and chocolate mixture in one
corner of the pastry, then fold over into
a triangle shape to enclose the filling.
Continue to fold in a triangular shape,
until the filo is completely wrapped
around the filling.

4 Dust the parcels with icing sugar
and cinnamon. Place on a baking
sheet and continue the process with
the remaining filo pastry and filling.

5 Bake in a preheated oven,
190°C/375°F/Gas Mark 5, for
about 15 minutes or until the little
pastries are golden. Remove from the
oven and serve hot – warn people
that the filling is very hot.

chocolate fudge pears

serves four

4 pears

1–2 tbsp lemon juice

300 ml/10 fl oz water

5 tbsp caster sugar

5-cm/2-inch piece of cinnamon stick

2 cloves

200 ml/7 fl oz double cream

125 ml/4 fl oz milk

140 g/5 oz light brown sugar

2 tbsp unsalted butter, diced

2 tbsp maple syrup

200 g/7 oz plain chocolate, broken
  into pieces

1 Peel the pears using a swivel vegetable peeler. Carefully cut out the cores from the base, but leave the stalks intact. Brush the pears with the lemon juice to prevent discoloration.

2 Pour the water into a large, heavy-based saucepan and add the caster sugar. Stir over a low heat until the sugar has dissolved. Add the pears, cinnamon and cloves and bring to the boil. (Add a little more water if the pears are not almost covered.) Lower the heat and simmer for 20 minutes.

3 Meanwhile, pour the cream and milk into another heavy-based saucepan and add the brown sugar, butter and maple syrup. Stir over a low heat until the sugar has dissolved and the butter has melted. Bring to the boil, then boil, stirring constantly, for 5 minutes, until thick and smooth. Remove from the heat and stir in the chocolate, a little at a time, waiting until each batch has melted before adding the next. Set aside.

4 Transfer the pears to serving plates. Bring the poaching syrup back to the boil and cook until reduced. Discard the cinnamon and cloves, then fold the syrup into the sauce. Pour over the pears and serve.

chocolate crêpes

serves six

85 g/3 oz plain flour

1 tbsp cocoa powder

1 tsp caster sugar

2 eggs, beaten lightly

175 ml/6 fl oz milk

2 tsp dark rum

140 g/5 oz unsalted butter

icing sugar, for dusting

FILLING

5 tbsp double cream

225 g/8 oz plain chocolate

3 eggs, separated

2 tbsp caster sugar

BERRY SAUCE

25 g/1 oz butter

4 tbsp caster sugar

150 ml/5 fl oz orange juice

225 g/8 oz berries, such as
   raspberries, blackberries and
   strawberries

3 tbsp white rum

1 To make the batter for the chocolate crêpes, sift the flour, cocoa and caster sugar into a bowl. Make a well in the centre and add the eggs, beating them in a little at a time. Add the milk and beat until smooth. Stir in the rum.

2 Melt all the butter and stir 2 tablespoonfuls into the batter. Cover with clingfilm and leave to stand for 30 minutes.

3 To cook the crêpes, brush the base of an 18-cm/7-inch pancake pan or non-stick frying pan with melted butter and set over a medium heat. Stir the batter and pour 3 tablespoonfuls into the pan, swirling it to cover the base. Cook for 2 minutes or until the underside is golden, flip over, cook for 30 seconds, then slide on to a plate. Cook another 11 crêpes in the same way. Stack the crêpes interleaved with baking paper.

4 For the filling, pour the cream into a heavy-based saucepan, add the chocolate and melt over a low heat, stirring. Remove from the heat. In a heatproof bowl, beat the egg yolks with half the sugar until creamy, beat in the chocolate cream and leave to cool.

5 Whisk the egg whites in a separate bowl until soft peaks form, add the rest of the sugar and beat into stiff peaks. Stir a spoonful of the whites into the chocolate mixture, then fold the mixture into the remaining egg whites.

6 Preheat the oven to 200°C/400°F/ Gas Mark 6. Brush a baking tray with melted butter. Spread 1 crêpe with 1 tablespoon of the filling, then fold it in half and in half again to make a triangle. Repeat with the remaining crêpes. Brush the tops with the remaining melted butter, place on the baking tray and bake for 20 minutes.

7 For the berry sauce, melt the butter in a frying pan over a low heat. Stir in the sugar and cook until golden. Stir in the orange juice and cook until syrupy. Add the berries and warm through, stirring gently. Add the rum, heat gently for 1 minute, then ignite with a long match. Shake the pan until the flames have died down. Transfer the flambéed crêpes to serving plates and dust with iciing sugar. Add a little of the sauce and serve immediately.

chocolate cranberry sponge

serves four

55 g/2 oz unsalted butter

4 tbsp dark brown sugar, plus 2 tsp
  extra for sprinkling

85 g/3 oz cranberries, defrosted
  if frozen

1 large cooking apple

2 eggs, beaten lightly

85 g/3 oz self-raising flour

3 tbsp cocoa powder

SAUCE

175 g/6 oz plain chocolate, broken
  into pieces

400 ml/14 fl oz evaporated milk

1 tsp vanilla essence

½ tsp almond essence

1 Grease a 1.2-litre/2-pint pudding basin, sprinkle with brown sugar to coat the sides and tip out any excess. Put the cranberries in a bowl. Peel, core and dice the apple and mix with the cranberries. Put the fruit in the prepared pudding basin.

2 Place the butter, brown sugar and eggs in a large bowl. Sift in the flour and cocoa and beat well until thoroughly mixed. Pour the mixture into the basin on top of the fruit, cover the top with foil and tie with string. Steam for about 1 hour, until risen, topping up with boiling water if necessary.

3 Meanwhile, to make the sauce, put the plain chocolate and milk into the top of a double boiler or a heatproof bowl set over a saucepan of barely simmering water. Stir until the chocolate has melted, then remove from the heat. Whisk in the vanilla and almond essences and continue to beat until the sauce is thick and smooth.

4 To serve, remove the pudding from the heat and discard the foil. Run a round-bladed knife around the side of the basin, place a serving plate on top of the pudding and, holding them together, carefully invert. Serve the sponge immediately, handing the sauce separately.

chocolate castle puddings

serves four

40 g/1½ butter

3 tbsp caster sugar

1 large egg, beaten lightly

85 g/3 oz self-raising flour

55 g/2 oz plain chocolate, melted

SAUCE

2 tbsp cocoa powder

2 tbsp cornflour

150 ml/5 fl oz single cream

300 ml/10 fl oz milk

1–2 tbsp dark brown sugar

1 Grease 4 dariole moulds or small heatproof bowls with butter. In a mixing bowl, cream the butter and sugar together until pale and fluffy. Gradually add the egg, beating well after each addition.

2 Sift the flour into a separate bowl, fold it into the butter mixture with a metal spoon. Stir in the melted chocolate. Divide the mixture among the moulds, filling them to about two-thirds full to allow for expansion during cooking. Cover each mould with a circle of foil, and tie securely in place with string.

3 Bring a large saucepan of water to the boil and set a steamer over it. Place the moulds in the steamer and cook for 40 minutes. Check the water level from time to time and top up with boiling water if necessary. Do not allow the saucepan to boil dry.

4 To make the sauce, put the cocoa powder, cornflour, cream and milk in a heavy-based pan. Bring to the boil, then lower the heat and simmer, whisking constantly, until thick and smooth. Cook for a further 2–3 minutes, then stir in brown sugar to taste. Pour the sauce into a jug.

5 Lift the moulds out of the steamer and remove the foil circles from them. Run a round-bladed knife around the sides of the moulds and turn out the puddings on to warmed, individual plates. Serve immediately, handing the sauce separately.

italian drowned ice cream

serves four

about 450 ml/16 fl oz freshly made
espresso coffee
chocolate-coated coffee beans, to
decorate
VANILLA ICE CREAM
1 vanilla pod
6 large egg yolks
150 g/5½ oz caster sugar, or vanilla-
flavoured sugar (sugar that has
been stored with a vanilla pod)
500 ml/18 fl oz milk
250 ml/9 fl oz plus 2 tbsp double
cream

1 To make the vanilla ice cream,
slit the vanilla pod lengthways
and scrape out the tiny brown seeds.
Set aside.

2 Put the yolks and sugar into a
heatproof bowl that will sit
over a saucepan with plenty of room
underneath it. Beat the egg yolks and
sugar together until thick and creamy.

3 Put the milk, cream and split
vanilla pods in the pan over a low
heat and bring to a simmer. Pour the
milk over the egg mixture, whisking.
Pour 2.5 cm/1 inch of water into a
saucepan. Place the bowl on top,
ensuring the base does not touch the
water. Turn the heat to medium-high.

4 Cook the mixture, stirring
constantly, until it is thick enough
to coat the back of the spoon. Remove
from the heat, transfer to a bowl and
leave to cool.

5 Churn the mixture in an
ice-cream maker, following
the manufacturer's instructions.
Alternatively, place it in a freezerproof
container and freeze for 1 hour, turn
out into a bowl and whisk to break
up the ice crystals, then return to
the freezer, repeating the process
4 times at 30-minute intervals.

6 Transfer the ice cream to a
freezerproof bowl, smooth the
top and cover with clingfilm or foil.
Freeze for up to 3 months.

7 Soften in the refrigerator for
20 minutes before serving.
Place scoops of ice cream in each
bowl. Pour over the coffee and
sprinkle with the coffee beans.

chocolate fruit dip

serves four

selection of fruit (choose from
 oranges, bananas, strawberries,
 pineapple chunks (fresh or
 canned), apricots (fresh or
 canned), eating apples, pears,
 kiwi fruit)
1 tbsp lemon juice
CHOCOLATE SAUCE
55 g/2 oz butter
50 g/1¾ oz plain chocolate, broken
 into small cubes
½ tbsp cocoa powder
2 tbsp golden syrup
BASTE
4 tbsp clear honey
grated rind and juice of ½ orange

1 To make the chocolate sauce,
place the butter, chocolate,
cocoa powder and golden syrup in
a small saucepan. Heat gently on the
hob or at the side of the barbecue,
stirring constantly, until all of the
ingredients have melted and are
well combined.

2 To prepare the fruit, peel and
core if necessary, then cut into
large, bite-sized pieces or wedges as
appropriate. Dip apples, pears and
bananas in lemon juice to prevent
discoloration. Thread the pieces of
fruit on to metal skewers.

3 To make the baste, mix the honey,
orange juice and rind together,
heat gently if required, and brush over
the fruit to cover completely.

4 Barbecue the fruit skewers over
warm coals for 5–10 minutes
until hot. Serve the skewers with the
chocolate dipping sauce.

chocolate fudge sauce

makes 225 ml/8 fl oz

150 ml/5 fl oz double cream

55 g/2 oz unsalted butter, diced

3 tbsp caster sugar

175 g/6 oz white chocolate, broken
   into pieces

2 tbsp brandy

1 Pour the cream into the top of a double boiler or a heatproof glass bowl set over a saucepan of barely simmering water. Add the butter and caster sugar and stir the mixture constantly with a wooden spoon until the mixture is smooth. Remove the pan from the heat.

2 Stir in the chocolate, a few pieces at a time, waiting until each batch has melted before adding the next. Add the brandy and stir the sauce until smooth. Leave the sauce to cool to room temperature before serving.

glossy chocolate sauce

makes 150 ml/5 fl oz

100 g/3½ oz caster sugar

4 tbsp water

175 g/6 oz plain chocolate, broken
into pieces

25 g/1 oz unsalted butter, diced

2 tbsp orange juice

1 Put the sugar and water into a small, heavy-based saucepan set over a low heat and stir until the sugar has dissolved. Stir in the chocolate, a few pieces at a time, waiting until each batch has melted before adding the next. Stir in the butter, a few pieces at a time, waiting until each batch has been incorporated before adding the next. Do not allow to boil.

2 Stir in the orange juice and remove the saucepan from the heat. Serve immediately or keep warm until required. Alternatively, leave to cool, transfer to a freezerproof container and freeze for up to 3 months. Thaw the sauce at room temperature before re-heating to serve.

french chocolate sauce

makes 150 ml/5 fl oz

6 tbsp double cream

85 g/3 oz plain chocolate, broken
   into small pieces

2 tbsp orange-flavoured liqueur

1 Bring the cream gently to the boil
   in a small, heavy-based saucepan
over a low heat. Remove the saucepan
from the heat, add the chocolate and
stir the sauce until smooth.

2 Stir in the orange-flavoured
   liqueur, transfer to a heatproof jug
and serve immediately. Alternatively, if
you prefer, keep the sauce warm
until required.

Cold Desserts

Cool, creamy, sumptuous and indulgent are just a few of the words that spring to mind when you think of cold chocolate desserts. The desserts contained in this chapter are a combination of all of these.

Some of the desserts are surprisingly quick and simple to make, while others are more elaborate. One of the best things about these desserts is they can all be made in advance, sometimes days before you need them, making them perfect for entertaining. A quick decoration when necessary is all that is needed on the day. Even the Baked Chocolate Alaska can be assembled in advance and popped into the oven just before serving.

iced white chocolate terrine

serves eight

2 tbsp granulated sugar

5 tbsp water

300 g/10½ oz white chocolate

3 eggs, separated

300 ml/10 fl oz double cream

COOK'S TIP

To make a coulis, place 225 g/
8 oz soft fruit, such as mangoes
or strawberries – in a food
processor or blender. Add 1–2
tablespoons of icing sugar and
blend to a purée. If the fruit
contains seeds, push the
purée through a sieve.

1 Line a 450-g/1-lb loaf tin with foil or clingfilm, pressing out as many creases as you can.

2 Place the granulated sugar and water in a heavy-based saucepan and heat gently, stirring until the sugar has dissolved. Bring to the boil and boil for 1–2 minutes until syrupy, then remove the saucepan from the heat.

3 Break the white chocolate into small pieces and stir it into the syrup, continuing to stir until the chocolate has melted and combined with the syrup. Leave to cool slightly.

4 Beat the egg yolks into the chocolate mixture. Leave to cool completely.

5 Lightly whip the cream until just holding its shape and fold it into the chocolate mixture.

6 Whisk the egg whites in a separate bowl until they are standing in soft peaks. Fold into the chocolate mixture. Pour into the prepared loaf tin and freeze overnight.

7 Remove from the freezer about 10–15 minutes before serving. Turn out of the tin, cut into slices and serve with a fruit coulis.

banana coconut cheesecake

serves ten

225 g/8 oz chocolate chip cookies

55 g/2 oz butter

350 g/12 oz medium fat soft cheese

75 g/2¾ oz caster sugar

50 g/1¾ oz fresh coconut, grated

2 tbsp coconut-flavoured liqueur

2 ripe bananas

125 g/4½ oz plain chocolate

1 sachet powdered gelatine

3 tbsp water

150 ml/5 fl oz double cream

TO DECORATE

1 banana

lemon juice

a little melted chocolate

COOK'S TIP

To crack the coconut, carefully pierce 2 of the 'eyes' and drain off all the liquid. Tap hard around the centre of the coconut with a hammer until it cracks; lever apart. Cut into slices or grate the flesh.

1 Place the biscuits in a plastic bag and crush with a rolling pin. Pour into a mixing bowl. Melt the butter and stir into the biscuit crumbs until well coated. Firmly press the biscuit mixture into the base and up the sides of a 20-cm/8-inch springform tin.

2 Beat the soft cheese and caster sugar together until well combined, then beat in the grated coconut and coconut-flavoured liqueur. Mash the bananas and beat them in. Melt the plain chocolate and beat into the mixture until well combined.

3 Sprinkle the gelatine over the water in a heatproof bowl and leave to go spongy. Place over a saucepan of hot water and stir until dissolved. Stir into the chocolate mixture. Whip the cream until just holding its shape and stir into the chocolate mixture. Spoon over the biscuit base and leave to chill in the refrigerator for 2 hours, until set.

4 To serve, carefully transfer to a serving plate. Slice the banana, toss in the lemon juice and arrange around the edge of the cheesecake. Drizzle with melted chocolate and leave to set.

chocolate rum pots

serves six

225 g/8 oz plain chocolate

4 eggs, separated

6 tbsp caster sugar

4 tbsp dark rum

4 tbsp double cream

TO DECORATE

a little whipped cream (optional)

marbled chocolate shapes

  (see page 140)

1 Melt the chocolate (see page 6) and leave to cool slightly.

2 Whisk the egg yolks and the caster sugar together in a bowl until pale and fluffy, using an electric mixer or balloon whisk.

3 Drizzle the chocolate into the mixture and fold in together with the rum and the double cream.

4 Whisk the egg whites in a separate bowl until standing in soft peaks. Fold the egg whites into the chocolate mixture in 2 batches. Divide the mixture between 6 ramekins, or other individual dishes, and leave to chill for at least 2 hours.

5 To serve, decorate each dish with a little whipped cream and marbled chocolate shapes.

chocolate hazelnut pots

serves six

2 eggs

2 egg yolks

1 tbsp caster sugar

1 tsp cornflour

600 ml/1 pint milk

75 g/3 oz plain chocolate

4 tbsp chocolate hazelnut spread

TO DECORATE

grated chocolate or quick chocolate
    curls (see page 7), to decorate

1 Beat the eggs, egg yolks, caster sugar and cornflour together until well combined. Heat the milk until almost boiling.

2 Gradually pour the milk on to the eggs, whisking as you do so. Melt the chocolate and hazelnut spread in a bowl set over a saucepan of gently simmering water, then whisk the melted chocolate mixture into the eggs.

3 Pour into 6 small ovenproof dishes and cover the dishes with foil. Place them in a roasting tin. Fill the tin with boiling water to come halfway up the sides of the dishes.

4 Bake in a preheated oven, 160°C/325°F/Gas Mark 3, for 35–40 minutes, until the custard is just set. Remove from the tin and cool, then chill until required. Serve decorated with grated chocolate or chocolate curls.

chocolate cheese pots

serves four

300 ml/10 fl oz low-fat natural
    fromage frais
150 ml/5 fl oz low-fat natural yogurt
2 tbsp icing sugar
4 tsp low-fat drinking chocolate
    powder
4 tsp cocoa powder
1 tsp vanilla essence
2 tbsp dark rum, optional
2 medium egg whites
4 chocolate decorations
    (see page 121)
TO SERVE
pieces of kiwi fruit, orange and
    banana
strawberries and raspberries

1 Mix the fromage frais and low-fat yogurt in a bowl. Sift in the sugar, drinking chocolate and cocoa powder and mix well.

2 Add the vanilla essence to the mixture and the rum (if using).

3 Whisk the egg whites, in a clean bowl, until stiff. Using a metal spoon, fold the egg whites into the chocolate mixture.

4 Spoon the fromage frais and chocolate mixture into 4 small china dessert pots or ramekins and leave to chill in the refrigerator for about 30 minutes.

5 Decorate each chocolate cheese pot with a chocolate decoration and serve with an assortment of fresh fruit, such as pieces of kiwi fruit, orange and banana, and a few whole strawberries and raspberries.

quick chocolate desserts

serves four

125 ml/4 fl oz water

4 tbsp caster sugar

175 g/6 oz plain chocolate, broken
into pieces

3 egg yolks

300 ml/10 fl oz double cream

dessert biscuits, to serve

1 Pour the water into a saucepan and add the sugar. Stir over a low heat until the sugar has dissolved. Bring to the boil and continue to boil, without stirring, for 3 minutes. Remove the saucepan from the heat and leave it to cool slightly.

2 Put the chocolate in a food processor and add the hot syrup. Process until the chocolate has melted, then add the egg yolks and process briefly until smooth. Finally, add the cream to the mixture and process until fully incorporated.

3 Pour the mixture into 4 glasses or individual bowls, cover with clingfilm and leave to chill in the refrigerator for 2 hours, until set. Serve with dessert biscuits of your choice.

champagne mousse

serves four

SPONGE

4 eggs

100 g/3½ oz caster sugar

75 g/2¾ oz self-raising flour

2 tbsp cocoa powder

25 g/1 oz butter, melted

MOUSSE

1 sachet gelatine

3 tbsp water

300 ml/10 fl oz champagne

300 ml/10 fl oz double cream

2 egg whites

6 tbsp caster sugar

55 g/2 oz plain chocolate-flavoured

cake covering, melted, to

decorate

1 Line a 38 x 25-cm/15 x 10-inch Swiss roll tin with greased baking paper. Place the eggs and sugar in a bowl and beat with an electric mixer until the mixture is very thick and the whisk leaves a trail when lifted. If using a balloon whisk, stand the bowl over a pan of hot water whilst whisking. Sift the flour and cocoa together and fold into the egg mixture. Fold in the butter. Pour into the tin and bake in a preheated oven, 200°C/400°F/Gas Mark 6, for 8 minutes or until springy to the touch. Cool for 5 minutes, then turn out on to a wire rack until cold. Meanwhile, line 4 10-cm/4-inch baking rings. Line the sides with 2.5-cm/1-inch strips of cake and the base with circles.

2 To make the mousse, sprinkle the gelatine over the water and leave to go spongy. Place the bowl over a saucepan of hot water and stir until dissolved. Stir in the champagne.

3 Whip the cream until just holding its shape. Fold in the champagne mixture. Leave in a cool place until on the point of setting, stirring. Whisk the egg whites until standing in soft peaks, add the sugar and whisk until glossy. Fold into the setting mixture. Spoon into the sponge cases, allowing the mixture to go above the sponge. Chill for 2 hours. Pipe the cake covering in squiggles on a piece of parchment, leave them to set, then use them to decorate the mousses.

black forest trifle

6 thin slices chocolate butter cream
   Swiss roll

800 g/1 lb 12 oz canned black
   cherries

2 tbsp kirsch

1 tbsp cornflour

2 tbsp caster sugar

425 ml/15 fl oz milk

3 egg yolks

1 egg

75 g/2¾ oz plain chocolate

300 ml/10 fl oz double cream,
   whipped lightly

TO DECORATE

plain chocolate caraque (see
   page 7)

maraschino cherries, optional

1 Place the slices of chocolate Swiss roll in the bottom of a glass serving bowl.

2 Drain the black cherries, reserving 6 tablespoons of the juice. Place the cherries and the reserved juice on top of the Swiss roll slices. Sprinkle the kirsch evenly over the cake and set aside.

2

3 Mix the cornflour and caster sugar in a bowl. Stir in enough of the milk to mix to a smooth paste. Beat in the egg yolks and the whole egg.

4 Heat the remaining milk in a small saucepan until almost boiling, then gradually pour it on to the egg mixture, whisking well until it is combined.

5 Place the bowl over a saucepan of hot water and cook over a low heat until the custard thickens, stirring. Add the chocolate and stir until melted.

6 Pour the chocolate custard over the cherries and cool. When cold, spread the cream over the custard, swirling with the back of a spoon. Chill before decorating.

6

7 Decorate with chocolate caraque and whole maraschino cherries (if using), before serving.

7

chocolate marquise

serves six

200 g/7 oz plain chocolate

100 g/3½ oz butter

3 egg yolks

75 g/2¾ oz caster sugar

1 tsp chocolate essence or 1 tbsp
   chocolate-flavoured liqueur

300 ml/10 fl oz double cream

TO SERVE

chocolate-dipped fruits (see page 54)

crème fraîche

cocoa powder, for dusting

1 Break the chocolate into pieces. Place the chocolate and butter in a bowl set over a saucepan of gently simmering water and stir until melted and well combined. Remove from the heat and leave to cool.

2 Place the egg yolks in a mixing bowl with the sugar and whisk until pale and fluffy. Using an electric mixer running on low speed, slowly whisk in the cool chocolate mixture. Stir in the chocolate essence or chocolate-flavoured liqueur.

3 Whip the cream until just holding its shape. Fold into the chocolate mixture. Spoon into 6 small ramekins or individual metal moulds. Leave to chill for at least 2 hours.

4 To serve, turn out the desserts on to individual serving dishes. If you have difficulty turning them out, dip the moulds into a bowl of warm water for a few seconds to help the marquise to slip out. Serve with chocolate-dipped fruits and crème fraîche and dust with cocoa powder.

chocolate mint swirl

serves six

300 ml/10 fl oz double cream

150 ml/5 fl oz creamy fromage frais

2 tbsp icing sugar

1 tbsp crème de menthe

175 g/6 oz plain chocolate

plain chocolate, to decorate

COOK'S TIP

Pipe the patterns freehand
or draw patterns on to baking
paper first, turn the parchment
over and then pipe the
chocolate, following the
drawn outline.

1 Place the cream in a large mixing bowl and whip it until standing in soft peaks.

2 Fold in the fromage frais and icing sugar, then place about one-third of the mixture in a smaller bowl. Stir the crème de menthe into the smaller bowl. Melt the plain chocolate in a bowl set over a saucepan of gently simmering water and stir it into the remaining mixture.

3 Place alternate spoonfuls of the 2 mixtures into serving glasses, then swirl the mixture together to give a decorative two-colour effect. Leave to cool and chill until required.

4 To make the piped chocolate decorations, melt a small amount of plain chocolate and place in a paper piping bag.

5 Place a sheet of baking paper on a board and pipe squiggles, stars or flower shapes with the melted chocolate. Alternatively, to make curved decorations, pipe decorations on to a long strip of baking paper, then carefully place the strip over a rolling pin, securing with sticky tape. Leave the chocolate to set, then carefully remove from the baking paper.

6 Decorate each dessert with piped chocolate decorations and serve. The desserts can be decorated and then chilled, if preferred.

chocolate banana sundae

serves four

GLOSSY CHOCOLATE SAUCE

55 g/2 oz plain chocolate

4 tbsp golden syrup

15 g/½ oz butter

1 tbsp brandy or rum, optional

SUNDAE

4 bananas

150 ml/5 fl oz double cream

8–12 scoops good-quality vanilla
  ice cream

75 g/2¾ oz flaked or chopped
  almonds, toasted

grated or flaked chocolate

4 fan wafer biscuits, to serve

1 To make the chocolate sauce, break the chocolate into small pieces and place in a heatproof bowl with the syrup and butter. Heat over a saucepan of hot water until melted, stirring. Remove from the heat and stir in the brandy or rum (if using).

2 Slice the bananas and whip the cream until just holding its shape. Place a scoop of ice cream in the bottom of 4 tall sundae dishes. Top with slices of banana, some chocolate sauce, a spoonful of cream and a good sprinkling of nuts.

3 Repeat the ice cream, banana and chocolate sauce layers, finishing with a good dollop of cream, sprinkled with nuts and a little grated or flaked chocolate. Serve the chocolate banana sundaes with fan wafer biscuits.

122

white chocolate ice cream

serves six

ICE CREAM

1 egg, plus 1 extra egg yolk

3 tbsp caster sugar

150 g/5½ oz white chocolate

300 ml/10 fl oz milk

150 ml/5 fl oz double cream

BISCUIT CUPS

1 egg white

4 tbsp caster sugar

2 tbsp plain flour, sifted

2 tbsp cocoa powder, sifted

25 g/1 oz butter, melted

plain chocolate, melted, to decorate

1 Place baking paper on 2 baking trays. To make the ice cream, beat the egg, egg yolk, and sugar. Break the chocolate into pieces, place in a bowl with 3 tablespoons of milk and melt over a saucepan of hot water. Heat the milk until almost boiling and whisk into the eggs. Place over a saucepan of simmering water and cook, stirring until the mixture thickens. Whisk in the chocolate. Cover with dampened baking paper and leave to cool.

2 Whip the cream until just holding its shape. Fold into the custard. Transfer to a freezer-proof container and freeze for 1–2 hours. Scrape into a bowl and beat again until smooth. Re-freeze until firm.

3 Beat the egg white and sugar. Beat in the flour and cocoa, then the butter. Place 1 tablespoon of mixture on 1 tray and spread out to a 13-cm/5-inch circle. Bake in a preheated oven, 200°C/400°F/Gas Mark 6, for 4–5 minutes. Remove and mould over an upturned cup. Leave to set, then cool. Repeat to make 6 cups. Serve the ice cream in the cups, drizzled with melted chocolate.

marble cheesecake

serves ten

BASE

225 g/8 oz toasted oat cereal

50 g/1¼ oz toasted hazelnuts, chopped

55 g/2 oz butter

25 g/1 oz plain chocolate

FILLING

350 g/12 oz full-fat soft cheese

100 g/3½ oz caster sugar

200 ml/7 fl oz thick yogurt

300 ml/10 fl oz double cream

1 sachet powdered gelatine

3 tbsp water

175 g/6 oz plain chocolate, melted

175 g/6 oz white chocolate, melted

1 Place the toasted oat cereal in a polythene bag and crush it roughly with a rolling pin. Pour the crushed cereal into a mixing bowl and stir in the toasted chopped hazelnuts.

2 Carefully melt the butter and chocolate together in a saucepan over a low heat and add to the cereal mixture, stirring until well coated.

3 Using the bottom of a glass, press the mixture into the base and up the sides of a 20-cm/8-inch springform tin.

4 Beat the cheese and sugar together with a wooden spoon until smooth. Beat in the yogurt. Whip the cream until just holding its shape and fold into the mixture. Sprinkle the gelatine over the water in a heatproof bowl and leave to go spongy. Place over a saucepan of hot water and stir until dissolved. Stir into the mixture.

5 Divide the soft cheese mixture in half and beat the plain chocolate into one half and the white chocolate into the other half.

6 Place alternate spoonfuls of mixture on top of the cereal base. Swirl the filling together with the tip of a knife to give a marbled effect. Smooth the top with a palette knife or a spatula. Chill the cheesecake for at least 2 hours to set before serving.

chocolate fruit tartlets

serves six

250 g/9 oz plain flour

3 tbsp cocoa powder

150 g/5½ oz butter

3 tbsp caster sugar

2–3 tbsp water

50 g/1¾ oz plain chocolate

50 g/1¾ oz chopped mixed nuts,
   toasted

350 g/12 oz prepared fruit

3 tbsp apricot jam or redcurrant jelly

VARIATION

If liked, you can fill the cases
with a little sweetened cream
before topping with the fruit.
For a chocolate-flavoured filling,
blend 225 g/8 oz chocolate
hazelnut spread with
5 tablespoons of thick yogurt or
whipped cream.

1 Sift the flour and cocoa powder into a mixing bowl. Cut the butter into small pieces and rub into the flour with your fingertips until the mixture resembles fine breadcrumbs.

2 Stir in the sugar. Add enough of the water to mix to a soft dough – about 1–2 tablespoons. Cover and chill for 15 minutes.

3 Roll out the pastry on a lightly floured work surface and use to line 6 tartlet tins, each 10 cm/4 inches across. Prick the pastry with a fork and line the pastry cases with crumpled foil. Bake in a preheated oven, 190°C/375°F/Gas Mark 5, for 10 minutes.

4 Remove the foil and bake for a further 5–10 minutes, until the pastry is crisp. Place the tins on a wire rack to cool completely.

5 Melt the chocolate. Spread out the chopped nuts on a plate. Remove the pastry cases from the tartlet tins. Spread melted chocolate on the rims, then dip in the nuts. Leave to set.

6 Arrange the fruit in the tartlet cases. Melt the apricot jam or redcurrant jelly with the remaining 1 tablespoon of water and brush it over the fruit. Chill the tartlets in the refrigerator until required.

chocolate cheesecake

serves twelve

100 g/3½ oz plain flour

100 g/3½ oz ground almonds

200 g/7 oz raw brown sugar

150 g/5½ oz margarine

675 g/1 lb 8 oz firm tofu, drained

175 ml/6 fl oz vegetable oil

125 ml/4 fl oz orange juice

175 ml/6 fl oz brandy

6 tbsp cocoa powder, plus extra
to decorate

2 tsp almond essence

TO DECORATE

icing sugar

Cape gooseberries

1 Put the flour, ground almonds and 1 tablespoon of the sugar in a bowl and mix well. Rub the margarine into the mixture to form a dough.

2 Lightly grease and line the base of a 23-cm/9-inch springform cake tin. Press the dough into the base of the tin to cover, pushing the dough right up to the edge of the tin.

3 Roughly chop the tofu and put in a food processor with the vegetable oil, orange juice, brandy, cocoa powder, almond essence and

remaining sugar and process until smooth and creamy. Pour the mixture over the base in the tin and smooth out using a palette knife. Cook in a preheated oven, 160°C/325°F/Gas Mark 3, for 1–1¼ hours or until set.

4 Leave to cool in the tin for 5 minutes, then remove from the tin and chill in the refrigerator. Dust with icing sugar and cocoa powder. Decorate the chocolate cheesecake with Cape gooseberries and serve.

tiramisù layers

serves six

150 ml/5 fl oz double cream

300 g/10½ oz plain chocolate

400 g/14 oz mascarpone cheese

400 ml/14 fl oz black coffee with
4 tbsp caster sugar, cooled

6 tbsp dark rum or brandy

36 sponge fingers,
about 400 g/14 oz

cocoa powder, for dusting

VARIATION

Try adding 50 g/1¾ oz toasted chopped hazelnuts to the chocolate mixture in Step 1, if you prefer.

1 Whip the cream until it just holds its shape. Melt the chocolate in a bowl over a pan of simmering water, stirring occasionally. Leave the chocolate to cool slightly, then stir into the mascarpone cheese and cream.

2 Mix the coffee and rum together in a bowl. Dip the sponge fingers into the mixture briefly so that they absorb the coffee and rum liquid but do not become soggy.

3 Place 3 sponge fingers on 3 serving plates.

4 Spoon a layer of the mascarpone and chocolate mixture over the sponge fingers.

5 Place 3 more sponge fingers on top of the mascarpone layer. Spread another layer of mascarpone and chocolate mixture and place 3 more sponge fingers on top.

6 Leave the tiramisù to chill in the refrigerator for at least 1 hour. Dust with a little cocoa powder just before serving.

129

strawberry cheesecake

serves eight

BASE

55 g/2 oz unsalted butter

225 g/8 oz crushed digestive
    biscuits

55 g/2 oz chopped walnuts

FILLING

450 g/1 lb mascarpone cheese

2 eggs, beaten

3 tbsp caster sugar

250 g/9 oz white chocolate, broken
    into pieces

225 g/8 oz strawberries, hulled and
    quartered

TOPPING

175 g/6 oz mascarpone cheese
chocolate caraque (see page 7)

16 whole strawberries

1 To make the base, melt the butter over a low heat and stir in the crushed biscuits and the nuts. Spoon the mixture into a 23-cm/9-inch loose-bottomed cake tin and press evenly over the base with the back of a spoon. Set aside.

2 Preheat the oven to 150°C/300°F/ Gas Mark 2. To make the filling, beat the cheese until smooth, then beat in the eggs and sugar. Put the chocolate in the top of a double boiler or in a heatproof bowl set over a saucepan of barely simmering water. Stir over a low heat until melted. Remove from the heat and cool slightly, then stir into the cheese mixture. Finally, stir in the strawberries.

3 Spoon the mixture into the cake tin, spread out evenly and smooth the surface. Bake in the preheated oven for 1 hour, until the filling is just firm. Turn off the oven but leave the cheesecake in it until completely cold.

4 Transfer the cheesecake to a serving plate and spread the mascarpone cheese on top. Decorate with chocolate caraque and whole strawberries.

chocolate brandy torte

serves twelve

BASE

250 g/9 oz gingernut biscuits

75 g/2¾ oz plain chocolate

100 g/3½ oz butter

FILLING

225 g/8 oz plain chocolate

250 g/9 oz mascarpone cheese

2 eggs, separated

3 tbsp brandy

300 ml/10 fl oz double cream

4 tbsp caster sugar

TO DECORATE

100 ml/3½ fl oz double cream

chocolate-coated coffee beans

3 Lightly whip the cream until just holding its shape and fold in the chocolate and cheese mixture.

4 Whisk the egg whites in a clean bowl until standing in soft peaks. Add the caster sugar a little at a time and whisk until thick and glossy. Fold into the chocolate mixture, in two batches, until just mixed.

5 Spoon the mixture into the base and chill for at least 2 hours. Transfer to a serving plate. To decorate, whip the cream and pipe rosettes on to the cheesecake, then add the chocolate-coated coffee beans.

1 Crush the biscuits in a polythene bag or in a food processor. Melt the chocolate and butter together and pour over the biscuits. Mix well, then use to line the base and sides of a 23-cm/9-inch loose-bottomed fluted flan tin or springform cake tin. Leave to chill whilst preparing the filling.

2 To make the filling, melt the chocolate in a saucepan, remove from the heat and beat in the mascarpone, egg yolks and brandy.

rich chocolate ice cream

serves six

ICE CREAM

1 egg

3 egg yolks

85 g/3 oz caster sugar

300 ml/10 fl oz full cream milk

250 g/9 oz plain chocolate

300 ml/10 fl oz double cream

TRELLIS CUPS

100 g/3½ oz plain chocolate

1 Beat the egg, egg yolks and caster sugar together in a mixing bowl until well combined. Heat the milk until it is almost boiling.

2 Gradually pour the hot milk on to the eggs, whisking as you do so. Place the bowl over a saucepan of gently simmering water and cook, stirring constantly until the custard mixture thickens sufficiently to thinly coat the back of a wooden spoon.

3 Break the chocolate into small pieces and add to the hot custard. Stir until the chocolate has melted. Cover with a sheet of dampened baking paper and leave to cool.

4 Whip the cream until just holding its shape, then fold into the cooled chocolate custard. Transfer to a freezerproof container and freeze for 1–2 hours, until the mixture is frozen 2.5 cm/1 inch from the sides.

5 Scrape the ice cream into a chilled bowl and beat again until smooth. Re-freeze until firm.

6 Meanwhile, make the trellis cups. Invert a muffin tray and cover 6 alternate mounds with clingfilm. Melt the chocolate, place it in a paper piping bag and snip off the end.

7 Pipe a circle around the base of the mound, then pipe chocolate back and forth over it to form a trellis; carefully pipe a double thickness. Pipe around the base again. Chill until set, then lift from the tray and remove the clingfilm. Serve the chocolate ice cream in the trellis cups.

chocolate freezer cake

serves eight

4 eggs

175 g/6 oz caster sugar

100 g/3½ oz self-raising flour

3 tbsp cocoa powder

500 ml/18 fl oz chocolate and mint
ice cream

Glossy Chocolate Sauce (see page
104)

1 Lightly grease a 23-cm/9-inch ring tin. Place the eggs and sugar in a large mixing bowl. If you are using an electric mixer, whisk the mixture until it is very thick and the whisk leaves a trail. If you are using a balloon whisk, stand the bowl over a saucepan of hot water whilst whisking.

2 Sift the flour and cocoa powder together and fold into the egg mixture. Pour into the prepared tin and bake in a preheated oven, 180°C/350°F/Gas Mark 4, for 30 minutes or until springy to the touch. Leave the cake to cool in the tin before turning out on to a wire rack to cool completely.

3 Rinse the cake tin and line with a strip of clingfilm, allowing it to overhang slightly. Carefully cut off the top 1 cm/½ inch of the cake in one slice and set aside.

4 Return the cake to the tin. Using a spoon, scoop out the centre, leaving a shell 1-cm/½-inch thick.

5 Remove the chocolate and mint ice cream from the freezer and leave to stand for a few minutes, then beat with a wooden spoon until softened a little. Fill the centre of the cake with the ice cream, smoothing the top. Replace the top of the cake.

6 Cover with the overhanging clingfilm and freeze for at least 2 hours.

7 To serve, turn the cake out on to a serving dish and drizzle over some of the Chocolate Sauce in an attractive pattern, if you wish. Cut the cake into slices to hand round and then serve the remaining chocolate sauce separately.

chocolate mousse

serves eight

100 g/3½ oz plain chocolate,
   melted

300 ml/10 fl oz natural yogurt

150 ml/5 fl oz Quark

4 tbsp caster sugar

1 tbsp orange juice

1 tbsp brandy

1½ tsp gelozone (vegetarian
   gelatine)

9 tbsp cold water

2 large egg whites

TO DECORATE

roughly grated dark and white
   chocolate

strips of orange rind

1 Put the melted chocolate, yogurt, Quark, sugar, orange juice and brandy in a food processor or blender and process for 30 seconds. Transfer the mixture to a large bowl.

2 Sprinkle the gelozone over the water and stir until dissolved.

3 Put the gelozone and water in a saucepan and bring to the boil, for 2 minutes. Cool the mixture slightly, then stir into the chocolate.

4 Whisk the egg whites until stiff peaks form and fold into the chocolate mixture using a metal spoon.

5 Line a 500-g/1 lb 2-oz loaf tin with clingfilm. Spoon the mousse into the tin. Chill in the refrigerator for 2 hours, until set. Turn the mousse out on to a serving plate and decorate with grated chocolate and orange rind.

chocolate charlotte

serves eight

about 22 sponge fingers

4 tbsp orange-flavoured liqueur

250 g/9 oz plain chocolate

150 ml/5 fl oz double cream

4 eggs

150 g/5½ oz caster sugar

TO DECORATE

150 ml/5 fl oz whipping cream

2 tbsp caster sugar

½ tsp vanilla essence

quick plain chocolate curls (see
    page 7)

chocolate decorations (see
    page 121), optional

1 Line the base of a Charlotte mould
or a deep 18-cm/7-inch round
cake tin with a piece of baking paper.

2 Place the sponge fingers on a tray
and sprinkle with half of the
orange-flavoured liqueur. Use to line
the sides of the mould or tin, trimming
if necessary to make a tight fit.

3 Break the chocolate into small
pieces, place in a bowl and melt
over a saucepan of hot water. Remove
from the heat and stir in the cream.

4 Separate the eggs and place
the whites in a large clean bowl.
Set aside. Beat the egg yolks into the
chocolate and cream mixture.

5 Whisk the egg whites until
standing in stiff peaks, then
gradually add the caster sugar,
whisking until stiff and glossy.
Carefully fold the egg whites into the
chocolate mixture in 2 batches,
taking care not to knock out all of the
air. Pour into the centre of the mould.
Trim the sponge fingers so that they
are level with the chocolate mixture.
Leave the Charlotte to chill in a
refrigerator for at least 5 hours.

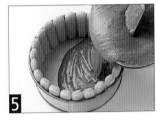

6 To decorate, whip the cream,
sugar and vanilla essence until
standing in soft peaks. Turn out the
Charlotte on to a serving plate. Pipe
cream rosettes around the base and
decorate with quick chocolate curls
and other decorations of your choice.

mocha swirl mousse

serves four

1 tbsp coffee and chicory essence

2 tsp cocoa powder, plus extra for
dusting

1 tsp low-fat drinking chocolate
powder

150 ml/5 fl oz low-fat crème fraîche,
plus 4 tsp to serve

2 tsp powdered gelatine

2 tbsp boiling water

2 large egg whites

2 tbsp caster sugar

4 chocolate-covered coffee beans,
to serve

1 Place the coffee and chicory essence in one bowl, and 2 teaspoons cocoa powder and the drinking chocolate in another bowl. Divide the crème fraîche between the 2 bowls and mix both well.

2 Dissolve the gelatine in the boiling water and set aside. Whisk the egg whites and sugar in a clean bowl until stiff and divide this evenly between the two mixtures.

3 Divide the dissolved gelatine between the 2 mixtures and gently fold in with a metal spoon.

4 Spoon small amounts of the 2 mousses alternately into 4 serving glasses and swirl together gently. Chill for 1 hour or until set.

5 To serve, top each mousse with a teaspoonful of crème fraîche, a chocolate coffee bean and a light dusting of cocoa powder.

138

layered chocolate mousse

serves four

3 eggs

1 tsp cornflour

4 tbsp caster sugar

300 ml/10 fl oz milk

1 sachet powdered gelatine

3 tbsp water

300 ml/10 fl oz double cream

75 g/2¾ oz plain chocolate

75 g/2¾ oz white chocolate

75 g/2¾ oz milk chocolate

chocolate caraque, to decorate (see

    page 7)

1 Line a 450-g/1-lb loaf tin with baking paper. Separate the eggs, putting each egg white in a separate bowl. Place the egg yolks, cornflour and sugar in a large mixing bowl and whisk until well combined. Place the milk in a saucepan and heat gently, stirring until almost boiling. Pour the milk on to the egg yolks, whisking.

2 Set the bowl over a saucepan of gently simmering water and cook, stirring until the mixture thinly coats the back of a wooden spoon.

3 Sprinkle the gelatine over the water in a small heatproof bowl and leave to go spongy. Place over a saucepan of hot water and stir until dissolved. Stir into the hot mixture. Leave to cool.

4 Whip the cream until just holding its shape. Fold into the egg custard, then divide the mixture into 3. Melt the 3 types of chocolate separately. Fold the plain chocolate into one egg custard portion. Whisk one egg white until standing in soft peaks and fold into the plain chocolate custard until combined. Pour into the

prepared tin and smooth the top. Chill in the coldest part of the refrigerator until just set. Leave the remaining mixtures at room temperature.

5 Fold the white chocolate into another portion of the egg custard. Whisk another egg white and fold in. Pour on top of the plain chocolate layer and chill quickly. Repeat with the remaining milk chocolate and egg white. Chill for at least 2 hours, until set. To serve, carefully turn out on to a serving dish and decorate with chocolate caraque.

chocolate & vanilla creams

serves four

450 ml/16 fl oz double cream

6 tbsp caster sugar

1 vanilla pod

200 ml/7 fl oz crème fraîche

2 tsp powdered gelatine

3 tbsp water

50 g/1¾ oz plain chocolate

MARBLED CHOCOLATE SHAPES

a little melted white chocolate

a little melted plain chocolate

1 Place the cream and sugar in a saucepan. Cut the vanilla pod into 2 pieces and add to the cream. Heat gently, stirring until the sugar has dissolved, then bring to the boil. Lower the heat and leave to simmer for 2–3 minutes.

2 Remove the saucepan from the heat and take out the vanilla pod. Stir in the crème fraîche.

3 Sprinkle the gelatine over the water in a small heatproof bowl and leave to go spongy, then place over a saucepan of hot water and stir until dissolved. Stir the gelatine into the cream mixture. Pour half of this mixture into another mixing bowl.

4 Melt the plain chocolate and stir it into one half of the cream mixture. Pour the chocolate mixture into 4 individual glass serving dishes and chill for 15–20 minutes until just set. While the chocolate mixture is chilling, keep the vanilla mixture at room temperature.

5 Take the serving dishes out of the refrigerator. Spoon the vanilla mixture on top of the chocolate mixture and chill again until the vanilla is set.

6 Meanwhile, make the shapes for the decoration. Spoon the melted white chocolate into a paper piping bag and snip off the tip. Spread some melted plain chocolate on a piece of baking paper. Whilst still wet, pipe a fine line of white chocolate in a scribble over the top. Use the tip of a cocktail stick to marble the white chocolate into the plain. When firm but not too hard, carefully cut into shapes with a small shaped cutter or a sharp knife. Chill the marbled chocolate shapes until firm, then use to decorate the desserts.

raspberry chocolate boxes

serves twelve

200 g/7 oz plain chocolate, broken
  into pieces

1½ tsp cold, strong black coffee

1 egg yolk

1½ tsp coffee liqueur

2 egg whites

200 g /7 oz fresh raspberries

SPONGE CAKE

1 egg, plus 1 egg white

4 tbsp caster sugar

5 tbsp plain flour

1. To make the mocha mousse, melt 55 g/2 oz of the chocolate in a heatproof bowl set over a saucepan of barely simmering water. Add the coffee and stir over a low heat until smooth, then remove from the heat and cool slightly. Stir in the egg yolk and the coffee liqueur.

2. Whisk the egg whites until standing in stiff peaks. Fold into the chocolate mixture, cover with clingfilm and chill for 2 hours, until set.

3. For the sponge cake, lightly grease a 20-cm/8-inch square cake tin and line the base with baking paper. Put the egg and extra egg white with the sugar in a heatproof bowl set over a saucepan of barely simmering water. Whisk for 5–10 minutes until pale and thick. Remove from the heat and continue whisking for 10 minutes until cold and the whisk leaves a ribbon trail when lifted.

4. Preheat the oven to 180°C/350°F/ Gas Mark 4. Sift the flour over the egg mixture and gently fold it in. Pour into the tin. Bake for 20–25 minutes, until firm to the touch and slightly shrunk from the sides of the tin. Turn out on to a wire rack to cool, then invert the cake, leaving the baking paper in place.

5. To make the boxes, grease a 30 x 23-cm/12 x 9-inch Swiss roll tin and line with greaseproof paper. Place the remaining chocolate in a heatproof bowl set over a saucepan of barely simmering water. Stir over a low heat until melted, but not too runny. Pour it into the tin and spread evenly. Leave in a cool place for about 30 minutes, until set.

6. Turn out the set chocolate. Using a ruler and sharp knife, cut it into 36 rectangles, measuring 7.5 x 2.5 cm/ 3 x 1 inches. Cut 12 of these in half to make 24 rectangles measuring 4 x 2.5 cm/1½ x 1 inches.

7. Trim the crusty edges off the sponge cake, then cut it into 12 slices, measuring 7.5 x 3 cm/3 x 1¼ inches. Spread a little of the set mocha mousse along the sides of each sponge rectangle and gently press 2 long and 2 short chocolate rectangles on each side to make boxes. Divide the remaining mousse among the boxes and top with raspberries.

mocha creams

serves four

225 g/8 oz plain chocolate

1 tbsp instant coffee

1 sachet powdered gelatine

300 ml/10 fl oz boiling water

3 tbsp cold water

1 tsp vanilla essence

1 tbsp coffee-flavoured liqueur,
   optional

300 ml/10 fl oz double cream

4 chocolate-covered coffee beans

8 amaretti biscuits, to serve

VARIATION

To add a delicious almond flavour to the dessert, replace the coffee-flavoured liqueur with almond-flavoured (Amaretto) liqueur.

1 Break the chocolate into small pieces and place in a saucepan with the coffee. Stir in the boiling water and heat gently, stirring until the chocolate melts.

2 Sprinkle the gelatine over the cold water and leave to go spongy, then whisk it into the hot chocolate mixture to dissolve it.

3 Stir in the vanilla essence and coffee-flavoured liqueur (if using). Leave the chocolate mixture to stand in a cool place until just beginning to thicken. Whisk from time to time.

4 Whisk the cream until standing in soft peaks, then reserve a little for decorating the desserts and fold the remainder into the chocolate mixture. Spoon the mixture into 4 tall glass serving dishes and leave to set.

5 Decorate with the reserved cream and coffee beans and serve with the amaretti biscuits.

banana cream profiteroles

serves four

CHOUX PASTRY

150 ml/5 fl oz water

60 g/2½ oz butter

85 g/3 oz strong plain flour, sifted

2 eggs

CHOCOLATE SAUCE

100 g/3½ oz plain chocolate,
    broken into pieces

2 tbsp water

4 tbsp icing sugar

25 g/1 oz unsalted butter

FILLING

300 ml/10 fl oz double cream

1 banana

2 tbsp icing sugar

2 tbsp banana-flavoured liqueur

1 Lightly grease a baking tray and sprinkle with a little water. To make the pastry, place the water in a pan. Cut the butter into small pieces and add to the pan. Heat gently until the butter melts, then bring to a rolling boil. Remove the pan from the heat and add the flour in one go, beating well until the mixture leaves the sides of the pan and forms a ball. Leave to cool slightly, then gradually beat in the eggs to form a smooth, glossy mixture.

Spoon the choux pastry mixture into a large piping bag fitted with a 1-cm/½-inch plain nozzle.

2 Pipe about 18 small balls of the choux pastry on to the baking tray, allowing enough room for them to expand during cooking. Bake in a preheated oven, 220°C/425°F/Gas Mark 7, for 15–20 minutes, until crisp and golden. Remove from the oven and, using a sharp knife, make a small slit in each one for steam to escape. Cool on a wire rack.

3 To make the chocolate sauce, place all the ingredients in a heatproof bowl set over a saucepan of simmering water and heat until combined to make a smooth, glossy sauce, stirring constantly.

4 To make the filling, whip the cream until standing in soft peaks. Mash the banana with the sugar and liqueur. Fold into the cream. Place in a piping bag fitted with a 1-cm/½-inch plain nozzle and carefully pipe into the profiteroles. Serve mounded up on a glass cake stand, with the chocolate sauce poured over.

1

2

cardamom cream horns

serves six

1 egg white

4 tbsp caster sugar

2 tbsp plain flour

2 tbsp cocoa powder

25 g/1 oz butter, melted

50 g/1¾ oz plain chocolate

CARDAMOM CREAM

150 ml/5 fl oz double cream

1 tbsp icing sugar

¼ tsp ground cardamom

pinch of ground ginger

25 g/1 oz stem ginger, chopped
    finely

1 Place a sheet of baking paper on 2 baking trays. Lightly grease 6 cream horn moulds. To make the horns, beat the egg white and sugar in a mixing bowl until well combined. Sift the flour and cocoa powder together, then beat into the egg white and sugar mixture, followed by the melted butter.

2 Bake 1 chocolate cone at a time. Place 1 tablespoon of the mixture on to 1 baking tray and spread out to form a 13-cm/5-inch circle. Bake in a preheated oven, 200°C/400°F/ Gas Mark 6, for 4–5 minutes.

3 Working quickly, remove the biscuit with a spatula and wrap around the cream horn mould to form a cone. Leave to set, then remove from the mould. Repeat with the remaining mixture to make 6 cones.

4 Melt the chocolate and dip the open edges of the horn in the chocolate. Place the horn on a piece of baking paper and leave to set.

5 To make the cardamom cream, place the cream in a bowl and sift the icing sugar and ground spices over the surface. Whisk the cream until standing in soft peaks. Fold in the chopped stem ginger and use to fill the chocolate cones.

chocolate shortcake towers

serves six

SHORTCAKE

225 g/8 oz butter

75 g/2¾ oz light muscovado sugar

50 g/1¾ oz plain chocolate, grated

275 g/9½ oz plain flour

COULIS

350 g/12 oz fresh raspberries

2 tbsp icing sugar

WHITE CHOCOLATE CREAM

300 ml/10 fl oz double cream

3 tbsp milk

100 g/3 oz white chocolate, melted

icing sugar, for dusting

1 Lightly grease a baking tray. To make the shortcake, beat the butter and sugar together until light and fluffy. Beat in the chocolate. Mix in the flour to form a stiff dough.

2 Roll out the dough on a lightly floured work surface and stamp out 18 rounds, 7.5-cm/3-inches across, with a fluted biscuit cutter. Place the rounds on the baking tray and bake in a preheated oven, 200°C/400°F/Gas Mark 6, for 10 minutes, until crisp and golden. Leave to cool on the tray.

3 To make the coulis, reserve about 100 g/3½ oz of the raspberries. Purée the remainder in a food processor with the icing sugar, then push through a sieve to remove the seeds. Chill. Reserve 2 teaspoons of the cream. Whip the remainder until just holding its shape. Fold in the milk and the melted chocolate.

4 For each tower, spoon a little coulis on to a serving plate. Drop small dots of the reserved cream into the coulis around the edge of the plate and use a skewer to drag through the cream to make an attractive pattern.

5 Place a shortcake circle on the plate and spoon on a little of the white chocolate cream. Top with 2 or 3 raspberries, then another shortcake circle and repeat. Place a third biscuit on top. Dust with icing sugar.

baked chocolate alaska

serves four

2 eggs

4 tbsp caster sugar

5 tbsp plain flour

2 tbsp cocoa powder

3 egg whites

150 g/5½ oz caster sugar

1 litre/1¾ pints good-quality
   chocolate ice cream

1 Grease an 18-cm/7-inch round cake tin and then line the base with baking paper.

2 Whisk the eggs and 4 tablespoons of the sugar in a mixing bowl until very thick and pale. Sift the flour and cocoa powder together and carefully fold in.

3 Pour into the prepared tin and bake in a preheated oven, 220°C/425°F/Gas Mark 7, for 7 minutes or until springy to the touch. Transfer the sponge to a wire rack to cool completely.

4 Whisk the egg whites in a clean bowl until standing in soft peaks. Gradually add the caster sugar, whisking until you have a thick, glossy meringue.

5 Place the sponge on a baking tray and pile the ice cream on to the centre in a heaped dome.

COOK'S TIP
This dessert is delicious served with a blackcurrant coulis. Cook a few blackcurrants in a little orange juice until soft, purée and push through a sieve, then sweeten to taste with a little icing sugar.

6 Pipe or spread the meringue over the ice cream, making sure the ice cream is completely enclosed. (At this point the dessert can be frozen, if wished.)

7 Return it to the oven for 5 minutes, until the meringue is just golden. Serve immediately.

chocolate orange sorbet

serves four

225 g/8 oz plain chocolate, broken
  into small pieces

1 litre/1¾ pints crushed ice

300 ml/10 fl oz freshly squeezed
  orange juice

150 ml/5 fl oz water

4 tbsp caster sugar

finely grated rind of 1 orange

juice and finely grated rind of
  1 lemon

1 tsp powdered gelatine

3 tbsp orange-flavoured liqueur

fresh mint sprigs, to decorate

1 Brush a 850-ml/1½-pint mould
with oil, drain well, then chill in
the refrigerator. Put the chocolate in
the top of a double boiler or into a
heatproof bowl set over a saucepan of
barely simmering water. Stir the
chocolate over a low heat until melted,
then remove from the heat.

2 Remove the mould from the
refrigerator and pour in the
melted chocolate. Tip and turn the
mould to coat the interior. Place the
mould on a bed of crushed ice and
continue tipping and turning until the
chocolate has set. Return the mould
to the refrigerator.

3 Reserve 3 tablespoons of the
orange juice in a small, heatproof
bowl. Pour the remainder into a
saucepan and add the water, sugar,
orange rind and lemon juice and rind.
Stir over a low heat until the sugar has
dissolved, then increase the heat and
bring the mixture to the boil. Remove
the saucepan from the heat.

4 Sprinkle the gelatine on the
reserved orange juice. Set aside
for 2 minutes to soften, then set over a
saucepan of barely simmering water
until dissolved. Stir the gelatine and
liqueur into the orange juice mixture.
Pour into a freezerproof container and
freeze for 30 minutes, until slushy.

5 Remove the sorbet from the
freezer, transfer it to a bowl and
beat thoroughly to break up the ice
crystals. Return it to the container and
freeze for 1 hour. Repeat this process
3 more times.

6 Remove the sorbet from the
freezer, and beat well. Remove
the mould from the refrigerator and
spoon the sorbet into it. Freeze
overnight. When ready to serve,
unmould the sorbet and decorate with
fresh mint sprigs.

chocolate & almond tart

serves eight

PASTRY

150 g/5 oz plain flour

2 tbsp caster sugar

125 g/4½ oz butter, cut into small
   pieces

1 tbsp water

FILLING

150 g/5½ oz golden syrup

55 g/2 oz butter

75 g/2¾ oz soft brown sugar

3 eggs, beaten lightly

100 g/3½ oz whole blanched
   almonds, chopped roughly

100 g/3½ oz white chocolate,
   chopped roughly

cream, to serve (optional)

1 To make the pastry, place the
flour and sugar in a mixing bowl
and rub in the butter with your
fingertips. Add the water and work the
mixture together until a soft pastry has
formed. Wrap and chill for 30 minutes.

2 Roll out the dough on a lightly
floured work surface and line a
24-cm/9½-inch loose-bottomed flan
tin. Prick the pastry with a fork and
leave to chill for 30 minutes. Line the

pastry case with foil and baking
beans and bake in a preheated
oven, 190°C/375°F/Gas Mark 5,
for 15 minutes. Remove the foil
and baking beans and cook for a
further 15 minutes.

3 Meanwhile, make the
filling. Gently melt the
syrup, butter and sugar together
in a saucepan. Remove from the
heat and leave to cool slightly.
Stir in the beaten eggs, almonds
and chocolate.

4 Pour the chocolate and nut
filling into the prepared
pastry case and cook in the oven
for 30–35 minutes or until just
set. Leave the tart to cool slightly
before removing the tart from
the tin. Serve with cream, if
wished.

chocolate pear tart

serves eight

PASTRY

115 g/4 oz plain flour

pinch of salt

2 tbsp caster sugar

115 g/4 oz unsalted butter, diced

1 egg yolk

1 tbsp lemon juice

TOPPING

115 g/4 oz plain chocolate, grated

4 pears

125 ml/4 fl oz single cream

1 egg, plus 1 egg yolk

½ tsp almond essence

3 tbsp caster sugar

1 To make the pastry, sift the flour and a pinch of salt into a mixing bowl. Add the sugar and butter and mix well with a pastry blender or 2 forks until thoroughly incorporated. Stir in the egg yolk and lemon juice to form a dough. Form the dough into a ball, wrap in clingfilm and chill in the refrigerator for 30 minutes.

2 Preheat the oven to 200°C/400°F/ Gas mark 6. Roll out the dough on a floured work surface and use to line a 25-cm/10-inch loose-bottomed flan tin. Sprinkle the grated chocolate over the base of the pastry case. Peel the pears, cut in half lengthways and remove the cores. Thinly slice each pear-half crossways and fan out the slices. Scoop up each pear-half with a spatula and arrange in the pastry case.

3 Beat the cream, egg, extra yolk and almond essence together and spoon the mixture over the pears. Sprinkle the sugar over the tart.

4 Bake in a preheated oven for 10 minutes. Lower the temperature to 180°C/350°F/Gas Mark 4 and bake for a further 20 minutes, until the pears are beginning to caramelise and the filling is just set. Leave to cool, then decorate with fresh mint sprigs and serve.

chocolate pecan pie

serves ten

PASTRY

280 g/10 oz plain flour

6 tbsp cocoa powder

115 g/4 oz icing sugar

pinch of salt

200 g/7 oz unsalted butter, diced

1 egg yolk

FILLING

85 g/3 oz plain chocolate, broken
   into small pieces

350 g/12 oz shelled pecan nuts

85 g/3 oz unsalted butter

175 g/6 oz brown sugar

3 eggs

2 tbsp double cream

2 tbsp plain flour

1 tbsp icing sugar, for dusting

1 To make the pastry, sift the flour, cocoa powder, sugar and salt into a mixing bowl and make a well in the centre. Put the butter and egg yolk in the well and gradually mix in the dry ingredients. Knead lightly into a ball. Cover with clingfilm and chill in the refrigerator for 1 hour.

2 Unwrap the dough and roll it out on a lightly floured work surface. Use it to line a 25-cm/10-inch non-stick springform pie tin and prick the base with a fork. Preheat the oven to 180°C/350°F/Gas Mark 4. Line the pastry case with baking paper and fill with baking beans. Bake in the preheated oven for 15 minutes. Remove from the oven, discard the beans and paper and leave the pastry base to cool.

3 To make the filling, put the chocolate in a heatproof bowl set over a saucepan of barely simmering water. Stir until melted. Remove from the heat and set aside. Roughly chop 225 g/8 oz of the pecans and set aside. Mix the butter with 55 g/2 oz of the brown sugar. Beat in the eggs, one at a time, then add the remaining brown sugar and mix well. Stir in the cream, flour, melted chocolate and chopped pecans.

4 Spoon the filling into the case. Cut the remaining pecans in half and arrange in circles over the pie.

5 Bake in the preheated oven for 30 minutes, then cover with foil. Bake for a further 25 minutes. Leave the pie to cool slightly before removing from the tin and transferring to a wire rack to cool completely. Dust with icing sugar.

155

mississippi mud pie

serves eight

225 g/8 oz plain flour

2 tbsp cocoa powder

150 g/5½ oz butter

2 tbsp caster sugar

about 2 tbsp cold water

FILLING

175 g/6 oz butter

350 g/12 oz dark muscovado sugar

4 eggs, beaten lightly

4 tbsp cocoa powder, sifted

150 g/5½ oz plain chocolate

300 ml/10 fl oz single cream

1 tsp chocolate essence

TOPPING

425 ml/15 fl oz double cream,
 whipped

chocolate flakes and quick chocolate
 curls (see page 7)

1 To make the pastry, sift the flour and cocoa powder into a mixing bowl. Rub in the butter with your fingertips until the mixture resembles fine breadcrumbs. Stir in the sugar and enough cold water to mix to a soft dough. Chill for 15 minutes.

2 Roll out the dough on a lightly floured work surface and use to line a deep 23-cm/9-inch loose-bottomed flan tin or ceramic flan dish. Line with foil or baking paper and baking beans. Bake blind in a preheated oven, 190°C/375°F/Gas Mark 5, for 15 minutes. Remove the beans and foil or paper and cook for a further 10 minutes, until crisp.

3 Meanwhile, make the filling. Beat the butter and sugar in a bowl and gradually beat in the eggs with the cocoa powder. Melt the chocolate and beat it into the mixture with the single cream and the chocolate essence.

4 Pour the mixture into the cooked pastry case and bake 160°C/325°F/Gas Mark 3, for 45 minutes or until the filling is set.

5 Leave to cool completely, then transfer the pie to a serving plate, if preferred. Cover with the whipped cream and leave to chill.

6 Decorate the pie with chocolate flakes and quick chocolate curls and chill before serving.

white chocolate moulds

serves six

125 g/4½ oz white chocolate,
  broken into pieces

250 ml/9 fl oz double cream

3 tbsp crème fraîche

2 eggs, separated

3 tbsp water

1½ tsp powdered gelatine

140 g/5 oz sliced strawberries

140 g/5 oz raspberries

140 g/5 oz blackcurrants

5 tbsp caster sugar

125 ml/4 fl oz crème de framboise

12 blackcurrant leaves, if available

1 Put the chocolate into the top of a double boiler or in a heatproof bowl set over a saucepan of barely simmering water. Stir over a low heat until melted and smooth. Remove from the heat and reserve.

2 Meanwhile, pour the cream into a saucepan and bring to just below boiling point over a low heat. Remove from the heat, then stir the cream and crème fraîche into the chocolate and cool slightly. Beat in the egg yolks, one at a time.

3 Pour the water into a small heatproof bowl and sprinkle the gelatine on the surface. Leave for 2–3 minutes to soften, then set over a saucepan of barely simmering water until completely dissolved. Stir the gelatine into the chocolate mixture and then leave until nearly set.

4 Brush the inside of 6 timbales, ramekins, dariole moulds or small cups with oil and line the bases with baking paper. Whisk the egg whites until soft peaks form, then fold them into the chocolate mixture. Divide the mixture evenly among the prepared

moulds and smooth the surface. Cover with clingfilm and chill in the refrigerator for 2 hours, until set.

5 Put the strawberries, raspberries and blackcurrants in a bowl and sprinkle with the caster sugar. Pour in the liqueur and stir gently to mix. Cover with clingfilm and then chill in the refrigerator for 2 hours.

6 To serve, run a round-bladed knife around the sides of the moulds and carefully turn out on to individual serving plates. Divide the fruit among the plates and serve immediately, decorated with blackcurrant leaves, if available.

chocolate sorbet

serves six

140 g/5 oz plain chocolate,
   chopped roughly
140 g/5 oz plain continental
   chocolate, chopped roughly
450 ml/16 fl oz water
200 g/7 oz caster sugar
langues de chat biscuits,
   to serve

1 Put both types of chocolate into a food processor and process briefly until very finely chopped.

2 Pour the water into a heavy-based saucepan and add the sugar. Stir over a medium heat to dissolve, then bring to the boil. Boil for 2 minutes, without stirring, then remove the saucepan from the heat.

3 With the motor of the food processor running, pour the hot syrup on to the chocolate. Process for about 2 minutes, until all the chocolate has melted and the mixture is smooth. Scrape down the sides of the food processor if necessary. Sieve the chocolate mixture into a freezerproof container and leave to cool.

4 When the mixture is cool, place it in the freezer for about 1 hour, until slushy, but beginning to become firm around the edges. Tip the mixture into the food processor and process until smooth. Return the sorbet to the container and freeze for at least 2 hours, until firm.

5 Remove the sorbet from the freezer about 10 minutes before serving and leave to stand at room temperature to soften slightly. Serve the chocolate sorbet in scoops and accompany with langues de chat biscuits.

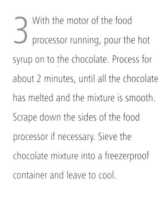

chocolate & honey ice cream

serves six

500 ml/18 fl oz milk

200 g/7 oz plain chocolate, broken
into pieces

4 eggs, separated

85 g/3 oz caster sugar

pinch of salt

2 tbsp clear honey

12 fresh strawberries, washed and
hulled

1 Pour the milk into a saucepan, add 150 g/5½ oz of the chocolate and stir over a medium heat for 3–5 minutes until melted. Remove the saucepan from the heat and reserve.

2 Beat the egg yolks with all but 1 tablespoon of the sugar in a separate bowl, until pale and thickened. Gradually, beat in the milk mixture, a little at a time. Return the mixture to a clean saucepan and cook over a low heat, whisking constantly, until smooth and thickened. Remove from the heat and leave to cool completely. Cover with clingfilm and chill in the refrigerator for 30 minutes.

3 Whisk the egg whites with a pinch of salt until soft peaks form. Gradually whisk in the remaining sugar and continue whisking until stiff and glossy. Remove the chocolate mixture from the refrigerator and stir in the honey, then, using a metal spoon, gently fold in the egg whites.

4 Divide the mixture among 6 individual freezerproof moulds and place in the freezer for at least 4 hours, until frozen. Meanwhile, put

the remaining chocolate into the top of a double boiler or in a heatproof bowl set over a saucepan of barely simmering water. Stir over a low heat until melted and smooth, then dip the strawberries in the melted chocolate so that they are half-coated. Leave to set on a sheet of baking paper. Transfer the ice cream to the refrigerator for 10 minutes before serving. Turn out on to serving plates and decorate with the strawberries.

marshmallow ice cream

serves four

85 g/3 oz plain chocolate, broken
    into pieces
175 g/6 oz white marshmallows
150 ml/5 fl oz milk
300 ml/10 fl oz double cream

1 Put the chocolate and marshmallows into a saucepan and pour in the milk. Warm over a very low heat until melted. Remove from the heat and leave the mixture to cool completely.

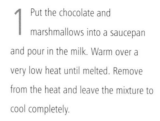

2 Whisk the cream until thick, then fold it into the cold chocolate mixture with a metal spoon. Pour into a 450-g/1-lb loaf tin and freeze for at least 2 hours, until firm (it will keep for 1 month in the freezer). Serve with fresh fruit.

chocolate & hazelnut parfait

serves six

175 g/6 oz blanched hazelnuts

175 g/6 oz plain chocolate, broken
  into small pieces

600 ml/1 pint double cream

3 eggs, separated

250 g/9 oz icing sugar

1 tbsp cocoa powder, for dusting

6 small fresh mint sprigs, to
  decorate

wafer biscuits, to serve

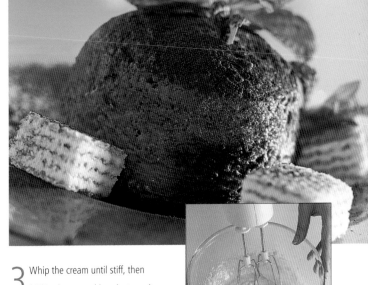

1 Spread out the hazelnuts on a baking tray and toast under a preheated medium hot grill, shaking the tray from time to time for about 5 minutes, until golden all over. Set aside to cool.

2 Put the chocolate into the top of a double boiler or in a heatproof bowl set over a saucepan of barely simmering water. Stir over a low heat until melted, then remove from the heat and cool. Put the toasted hazelnuts in a food processor and process until finely ground.

3 Whip the cream until stiff, then fold in the ground hazelnuts and set aside. Beat the egg yolks with 3 tablespoons of the sugar for 10 minutes until pale and thick.

4 Whisk the egg whites in a clean bowl until soft peaks form. Whisk in the remaining sugar, a little at a time, until the whites are stiff and glossy. Stir the cooled chocolate into the egg yolk mixture, then fold in the cream, and finally, fold in the egg whites. Divide the mixture among 6 freezerproof timbales or moulds, cover with clingfilm and freeze for at least 8 hours or overnight until firm.

5 Transfer the parfaits to the refrigerator about 10 minutes before serving to soften slightly. Turn out on to individual serving plates, dust the tops lightly with cocoa powder, decorate with fresh mint sprigs and serve with wafers.

mint-chocolate gelato

serves four

6 large eggs

150 g/5½ oz caster sugar

300 ml/10 fl oz milk

150 ml/5 fl oz double cream

large handful of fresh mint leaves,
 rinsed and dried

2 drops green food colouring,
 optional

55 g/2 oz plain chocolate, chopped
 finely

1 Put the eggs and sugar into a heatproof bowl that will sit over a saucepan with plenty of room underneath. Using an electric mixer, beat the eggs and sugar together until thick and creamy.

2 Put the milk and cream in the saucepan and bring to a simmer, (where small bubbles appear all around the edge), stirring. Pour on to the eggs, whisking constantly. Rinse the saucepan and put 2.5 cm/1 inch of water in the base. Place the bowl on top, making sure the base does not touch the water. Turn the heat to medium-high.

3 Transfer the mixture to a saucepan and cook, stirring constantly with a wooden spoon, until the mixture is thick enough to coat the back of the spoon and leave a mark when you pull your finger across it.

4 Tear the mint leaves and stir them into the custard. Remove from the heat. Leave to cool, then cover and infuse for at least 2 hours, chilling for the last 30 minutes.

5 Sieve the mixture through a small nylon sieve, to remove the pieces of mint. Stir in the food colouring (if using). Transfer to a freezerproof container and freeze the mixture for 1–2 hours until frozen 2.5 cm/1 inch from the sides of the container.

6 Scrape into a bowl and beat again until smooth. Stir in the chopped chocolate, smooth the top and cover with clingfilm or foil. Freeze until set, for up to 3 months. Soften the ice cream in the refrigerator for 20 minutes before serving.

chocolate rice dessert

serves eight

100 g/3½ oz long-grain white rice

pinch of salt

600 ml/1 pint milk

100 g/3½ oz granulated sugar

200 g/7 oz continental plain or plain
    chocolate, chopped

70 g/2½ oz butter, diced

1 tsp vanilla essence

2 tbsp brandy or Cognac

175 ml/6 fl oz double cream

whipped cream, for piping
    (optional)

quick chocolate curls (see page 7),
    to decorate (optional)

VARIATION

To mould the chocolate rice,
soften 1 sachet of gelatine in
about 50 ml/2 fl oz of cold water
and heat gently until dissolved.
Stir into the chocolate just before
folding in the cream. Pour into
a rinsed mould, leave to set,
then unmould.

1 Bring a saucepan of water to the boil. Sprinkle in the rice and add the salt. Reduce the heat and simmer gently for 15–20 minutes, until the rice is just tender. Drain the rice, rinse and drain once again.

2 Heat the milk and the sugar in a large heavy-based saucepan over a medium heat until the sugar dissolves, stirring frequently. Add the chocolate and butter and stir until melted and smooth.

3 Stir in the cooked rice and reduce the heat to low. Cover and simmer, stirring occasionally, for 30 minutes, until the milk is absorbed and the mixture thickened. Stir in the vanilla essence and brandy. Remove from the heat and leave to cool to room temperature.

4 Using an electric mixer, whip the cream until soft peaks form. Stir one heaped spoonful of the cream into the chocolate rice mixture to lighten it then fold in the remaining cream.

5 Spoon the mixture into glass serving dishes, cover and chill for about 2 hours. If wished, decorate with piped whipped cream and top with quick chocolate curls.

zuccotto

600 ml/1 pint double cream

2 tbsp icing sugar

55 g/2 oz hazelnuts, toasted

225 g/8 oz cherries, halved and
    stoned

115 g/4 oz plain chocolate,
    chopped finely

2 x 20-cm/8-inch round chocolate
    sponge cakes

4 tbsp brandy

4 tbsp Amaretto liqueur

TO DECORATE

2 tbsp icing sugar

2 tbsp cocoa powder

1 Whip the cream in a large bowl, until stiff, then fold in the sugar, followed by the toasted hazelnuts, cherries and chocolate. Cover the cream mixture with clingfilm and leave to chill in the refrigerator until required.

2 Meanwhile, cut the cakes in half horizontally and then cut the pieces to fit a 1.2-litre/2-pint pudding basin, so that the base and sides are completely lined. Reserve the remaining sponge cake. Mix the brandy and Amaretto liqueur together in a small bowl and sprinkle the mixture evenly over the sponge cake lining so it can soak in.

3 Remove the cream filling from the refrigerator and spoon it into the lined basin. Cover the top with the remaining sponge cake, cut to fit. Cover with clingfilm and chill in the refrigerator for 2 hours or until ready to serve.

4 For the decoration, sift the icing sugar and cocoa powder into separate bowls. Remove the zucotto from the refrigerator and run a round-bladed knife around the sides to gently loosen it. Place a serving plate on top of the basin and unmould. Dust alternate quarters of the zuccotto with icing sugar and cocoa powder.

zuccherini

serves six

175 g/6 oz plain chocolate, broken
    into pieces

10 amaretti biscuits, crushed

MOUSSE

55 g/2 oz plain chocolate, broken
    into pieces

1 tbsp cold, strong black coffee

2 eggs, separated

2 tsp orange-flavoured liqueur

TO DECORATE

150 ml/5 fl oz double cream

2 tbsp cocoa powder

6 chocolate-coated coffee beans

1 To make the chocolate cups to hold the filling, put the plain chocolate into the top of a double boiler or in a heatproof bowl set over a saucepan of barely simmering water. Stir until melted and smooth, but not too runny, then remove the chocolate from the heat. Carefully and evenly coat the inside of 12 double paper cake cases with melted chocolate, using a small brush. Stand the chocolate cups on a tray and chill for at least 8 hours or overnight in the refrigerator.

2 To make the mousse, put the chocolate and coffee into the top of a double boiler or in a heatproof bowl set over a saucepan of barely simmering water. Stir over a low heat until the chocolate has melted and the mixture is smooth, then remove from the heat. Cool slightly, then stir in the egg yolks and liqueur.

3 Whisk the egg whites in a separate bowl until stiff peaks form. Fold the whites into the chocolate mixture with a metal spoon, then leave to cool.

4 Remove the chocolate cups from the refrigerator and carefully peel off the paper cases. Divide the crushed amaretti biscuits equally among the

chocolate cups and top with the chocolate mousse. Return to the refrigerator for at least 30 minutes. Just before serving, whip the cream and pipe a star on the top of each chocolate cup. Dust half of the zuccherini with cocoa powder and then decorate the other half with the chocolate-coated coffee beans.

filo nests

serves four

15 g/½ oz unsalted butter

6 sheets filo pastry, about
    30 x 15 cm/12 x 6 inches each

40 g/1½ oz plain chocolate, broken
    into pieces

115 g/4 oz ricotta cheese

16 seedless green grapes, halved

24 seedless black grapes, halved

1 Put the butter into a small saucepan and set over a low heat until melted. Remove from the heat. Preheat the oven to 190°C/375°F/ Gas Mark 5. Cut each sheet of pastry into 4, to give 24 rectangles, each measuring about 15 x 7.5 cm/ 6 x 3 inches, then stack them all on top of each other. Brush 4 shallow tartlet tins with melted butter. Line 1 tin with a rectangle of pastry, brush with melted butter, and place another rectangle on top at an angle to the first and brush it with melted butter. Continue in this way, lining each tin with 6 rectangles, each brushed with melted butter. Brush the top layers of the pastry nests with melted butter.

2 Bake in a preheated oven for 7–8 minutes, until golden and crisp. Remove the pastry nests from the oven and leave to cool in the tins.

3 Put the chocolate into the top of a double boiler or into a heatproof bowl set over a saucepan of barely simmering water. Stir over a low heat until melted. Remove from the heat and cool slightly. Brush the insides of the pastry nests with about half the melted chocolate. Beat the ricotta until smooth, then beat in the remaining melted chocolate.

4 Divide the chocolate ricotta mixture evenly among the pastry cases and arrange the green and black grapes alternately around the edges. Carefully lift the filled pastry nests out of the tins and serve immediately.

chocolate & pernod creams

serves four

55 g/2 oz plain chocolate, broken
  into pieces
250 ml/9 fl oz milk
300 ml/10 fl oz double cream
2 tbsp caster sugar
1 tbsp arrowroot dissolved in
  2 tbsp milk
3 tbsp Pernod
langues de chat biscuits, or
  chocolate-tipped rolled wafers,
  to serve

1 Put the chocolate into the top of a double boiler or in a heatproof bowl set over a saucepan of barely simmering water. Stir over a low heat until melted. Remove from the heat and leave to cool slightly.

2 Pour the milk and cream into a saucepan over a low heat and bring to just below boiling point, stirring occasionally. Remove the saucepan from the heat and then set aside.

3 Beat the sugar and the arrowroot mixture into the melted chocolate. Gradually stir in the hot milk and cream mixture, then stir in the Pernod. Return the double boiler to the heat or set the bowl over a saucepan of barely simmering water and cook, over a low heat, for 10 minutes, stirring constantly, until thick and smooth. Remove the chocolate and Pernod from the heat and then set aside to cool.

4 Pour the chocolate and Pernod mixture into 4 individual serving glasses. Cover with clingfilm and chill in the refrigerator for 2 hours. Serve the chocolate and Pernod creams with langues de chats biscuits or chocolate-tipped rolled wafers.

small cakes & cookies

This chapter contains everyday delights for chocolate fans. You are sure to be tempted by our wonderful array of cookies and small cakes. Make any day special with a home-made chocolate biscuit to be served with coffee, as a snack or to accompany a special dessert. Although some take a little longer to make, most are quick and easy to prepare and decoration is often simple although you can get carried away if you like!

You'll find recipes for old favourites, such as Chocolate Chip Muffins and Chocolate Chip Cookies, Chocolate Butterfly Cakes and Chocolate Brownies. There are also new recipes for biscuits and small cakes, such as Chocolate Coconut Squares or Malted Chocolate Wedges. Finally, we have given the chocolate treatment to some traditional recipes – try Chocolate Scones or Chocolate Chip Flapjacks.

chocolate rum babas

serves four

100 g/3½ oz strong plain flour

2 tbsp cocoa powder

1 sachet easy-blend dried yeast

pinch of salt

1 tbsp caster sugar

40 g/1½ oz plain chocolate, grated

2 eggs

3 tbsp tepid milk

55 g/2 oz butter, melted

SYRUP

4 tbsp clear honey

2 tbsp water

4 tbsp rum

TO SERVE

whipped cream

cocoa powder, for dusting

fresh fruit, optional

1 Lightly oil 4 individual ring tins. Sift the flour and cocoa powder together in a large warmed mixing bowl. Stir in the yeast, salt, sugar and grated chocolate. Beat the eggs together in a separate bowl, add the milk and butter, and beat until mixed.

2 Make a well in the centre of the dry ingredients and pour in the egg mixture, beating to mix to a batter. Beat for 10 minutes, ideally in a electric mixer with a dough hook. Divide the mixture between the tins – it should come halfway up the sides.

3 Place on a baking tray and cover with a damp tea towel. Leave in a warm place until the mixture rises almost to the tops of the tins. Bake in a preheated oven, 200°C/400°F/Gas Mark 6, for 15 minutes.

4 To make the syrup, gently heat all of the ingredients together in a small saucepan. Turn out the babas and place on a wire rack placed above a tray to catch the syrup. Drizzle the syrup over the babas and leave for at least 2 hours to allow the syrup to soak in. Once or twice, spoon the syrup that has dripped on to the tray over the babas.

5 Fill the centre of the babas with whipped cream and dust with cocoa powder. Serve the babas with fresh fruit, if wished.

chocolate fudge brownies

makes sixteen

200 g/7 oz low-fat soft cheese

½ tsp vanilla essence

250 g/9 oz caster sugar

2 eggs

100 g/3½ oz butter

3 tbsp cocoa powder

100 g/3½ oz self-raising flour, sifted

50 g/1¾ oz pecans, chopped

FUDGE ICING

55 g/2 oz butter

1 tbsp milk

100 g/3½ oz icing sugar

2 tbsp cocoa powder

pecan nuts, to decorate (optional)

1 Lightly grease a 20-cm/8-inch square shallow cake tin and line the base with baking paper.

2 Beat the cheese, vanilla essence and 25 g/1 oz of the caster sugar together until smooth, then set aside.

3 Beat the eggs and remaining caster sugar together until light and fluffy. Place the butter and cocoa powder in a small saucepan and heat gently, stirring until the butter melts and the mixture combines, then stir it into the egg mixture. Fold in the flour and nuts.

4 Pour half of the brownie mixture into the tin and smooth the top. Carefully spread the soft cheese over it, then cover it with the remaining brownie mixture. Bake in a preheated oven, 180°C/350°F/Gas Mark 4, for 40–45 minutes. Cool in the tin.

5 To make the fudge icing, melt the butter in the milk. Stir in the icing sugar and cocoa powder. Using a palette knife, spread the icing over the brownies and decorate with pecan nuts (if using). Leave the icing to set, then cut into squares to serve.

VARIATION

Omit the cheese layer if preferred. Use walnuts in place of the pecan nuts.

pain au chocolat

makes twelve

450 g/1 lb strong plain flour

½ tsp salt

1 sachet easy-blend dried yeast

25 g/1 oz white vegetable fat

1 egg, beaten lightly

225 ml/8 fl oz tepid water

175 g/6 oz butter, softened

100 g/3½ oz plain chocolate,
    broken into 12 squares

beaten egg, for glazing

icing sugar, for dusting

1 Lightly grease a baking tray with a little butter. Set aside. Sift the flour and salt into a mixing bowl and stir in the easy-blend dried yeast. Rub the white vegetable fat into the flour and yeast mixture with your fingertips. Add the egg and enough of the water to mix to a soft dough. Knead it for about 10 minutes to make a smooth, elastic dough.

2 Roll the dough out to form a rectangle measuring 38 x 20 cm/ 15 x 8 inches. Divide the butter into 3 portions and dot 1 portion over two-thirds of the rectangle, leaving a small border around the edge.

3 Fold the rectangle into 3 by first folding the plain part of the dough over and then the other side. Seal the edges of the dough by pressing with a rolling pin. Give the dough a quarter turn so the sealed edges are at the top and bottom. Re-roll and fold (without adding butter), then wrap the dough in clingfilm and leave to chill in the refrigerator for 30 minutes.

4 Repeat steps 2 and 3 until all of the butter has been used, chilling the dough each time. Re-roll and fold the dough twice more without butter. Chill for a final 30 minutes.

5 Roll out the dough to a rectangle measuring 46 x 30 cm/18 x 12 inches, trim, and halve lengthways. Cut each half into 6 rectangles and brush with beaten egg. Place a chocolate square at one end of each rectangle and roll up to form a sausage. Press the ends together and place, seam-side down, on the baking tray. Cover and leave to rise for 40 minutes in a warm place. Brush with egg and bake in a preheated oven, 220°C/425°F/Gas Mark 7, for 20–25 minutes until golden. Cool on a wire rack. Serve warm or cold.

chocolate dairy wraps

serves six

2 eggs

4 tbsp caster sugar

6 tbsp plain flour

1½ tbsp cocoa powder

4 tbsp apricot jam

150 ml/5 fl oz double cream,
  whipped

icing sugar, for dusting

1 Line 2 baking trays with pieces of baking paper. Whisk the eggs and sugar together until the mixture is very light and fluffy and the whisk leaves a trail when lifted.

2 Sift the flour and cocoa powder together. Using a metal spoon or a spatula, gently fold it into the eggs and sugar in a figure-of-eight movement.

3 Drop rounded tablespoons of the mixture on to the lined baking trays and spread them into oval shapes. Make sure the ovals are well spaced apart as they will spread out during cooking.

4 Bake in a preheated oven, 220°C/425°F/Gas Mark 7, for 6–8 minutes or until springy to the touch. Leave to cool on the baking trays.

5 When cold, slide the cakes on to a damp tea towel and leave to stand until cold. Carefully remove them from the dampened paper. Spread the flat side of the cakes with jam, then spoon or pipe the whipped cream down the centre of each one.

6 Fold the chocolate dairy wraps in half and place them on a serving plate. Sprinkle them with a little icing sugar and serve.

no-bake chocolate squares

1

2

4

makes sixteen

275 g/9½ oz plain chocolate

175 g/6 oz butter

4 tbsp golden syrup

2 tbsp dark rum, optional

175 g/6 oz plain biscuits, such as
Rich Tea

25 g/1 oz toasted rice cereal

50 g/1¾ oz chopped walnuts or
pecan nuts

100 g/3½ oz glacé cherries,
chopped roughly

25 g/1 oz white chocolate, to
decorate

1 Place the plain chocolate in a
large mixing bowl with the butter,
syrup and rum (if using) and set over a
saucepan of gently simmering water
until melted, stirring until blended.

2 Break the biscuits into small
pieces and stir them into the
chocolate mixture along with the rice
cereal, nuts and glacé cherries.

3 Line an 18-cm/7-inch square cake
tin with baking paper. Pour the
mixture into the tin and smooth the
top, pressing down well with the back
of a spoon. Chill for 2 hours.

4 To decorate, melt the white
chocolate and drizzle it over the
top of the cake in a random pattern.
Leave to set. To serve, carefully turn
out of the tin and remove the baking
paper. Cut into 16 squares.

VARIATION

Brandy or an orange-flavoured
liqueur can be used instead of
the rum, if you prefer. Cherry
brandy also works well.

chocolate butterfly cakes

makes twelve

125 g/4½ oz soft margarine

125 g/4½ oz caster sugar

150 g/5½ oz self-raising flour

2 large eggs

2 tbsp cocoa powder

25 g/1 oz plain chocolate, melted

LEMON BUTTER CREAM

100 g/3½ oz unsalted butter,
    softened

225 g/8 oz icing sugar, sifted

grated rind of ½ lemon

1 tbsp lemon juice

icing sugar, for dusting

1 Place 12 paper cases in a bun tray. Place all of the ingredients for the cakes, except for the melted chocolate, in a large mixing bowl and beat with an electric mixer until the mixture is just smooth. Beat in the melted chocolate.

2 Spoon equal amounts of the cake mixture into each paper case, filling them three-quarters full. Bake in a preheated oven, 180°C/350°F/Gas Mark 4, for 15 minutes or until springy to the touch. Transfer the chocolate cakes to a wire rack and leave them to cool completely.

3 Meanwhile, make the lemon butter cream. Place the butter in a mixing bowl and beat until fluffy, then gradually beat in the icing sugar. Beat in the lemon rind and gradually add the lemon juice, beating well.

4 When cold, cut the top off each cake using a serrated knife. Cut each cake top in half.

5 Spread or pipe the butter cream over the cut surface of each cake and push the 2 cut pieces of cake top into the icing to form wings. Sprinkle the cakes with icing sugar.

chocolate scones

serves four

225 g/8 oz self-raising flour, sifted

5 tbsp butter, diced

1 tbsp caster sugar

50 g/1¾ oz chocolate chips

about 150 ml/5 fl oz milk

COOK'S TIP

To be at their best, all scones
should be freshly baked and
served warm. Split the scones
and spread with chocolate
hazelnut spread.

1 Lightly grease a baking tray. Place the flour in a mixing bowl. Rub the butter into the flour with your fingertips until the scone mixture resembles fine breadcrumbs.

2 Stir in the caster sugar and chocolate chips.

3 Mix in enough milk to form a soft dough.

4 On a lightly floured work surface, roll out the dough to form a rectangle measuring 10 x 15 cm/4 x 6 inches, about 2.5-cm/1-inch thick. Cut the dough into 9 squares.

5 Place the scones, spaced well apart, on the prepared baking tray.

6 Brush with a little milk and bake in a preheated oven, 220°C/425°F/ Gas Mark 7, for 10–12 minutes, until the scones are risen and golden. Serve the scones warm.

chocolate crispy bites

makes sixteen

WHITE CHOCOLATE LAYER

55 g/2 oz butter

1 tbsp golden syrup

150 g/5½ oz white chocolate

50 g/1¾ oz toasted rice cereal

PLAIN CHOCOLATE LAYER

55 g/2 oz butter

2 tbsp golden syrup

125 g/4½ oz plain chocolate,
    broken into small pieces

75 g/2¾ oz toasted rice cereal

COOK'S TIP

These bites can be made up
to 4 days ahead. Keep them
covered in the refrigerator
until ready to use.

1 Grease a 20-cm/8-inch square cake tin with a little butter and line with baking paper.

2 To make the white chocolate layer, melt the butter, golden syrup and chocolate in a bowl set over a saucepan of gently simmering water.

3 Remove from the heat and stir in the toasted rice cereal until it is well combined.

4 Press into the prepared tin and smooth the surface.

5 To make the plain chocolate layer, melt the butter, golden syrup and plain chocolate in a bowl set over a saucepan of gently simmering water.

6 Remove from the heat and stir in the toasted rice cereal. Pour the plain chocolate layer over the hardened white chocolate layer, and chill in the refrigerator until hardened.

7 Turn the mixture out of the cake tin and carefully cut into small squares using a sharp knife.

chocolate coconut squares

makes nine

225 g/8 oz plain chocolate digestive
 biscuits

85 g/3 oz butter or margarine

175 g/6 oz canned evaporated milk

1 egg, beaten

1 tsp vanilla essence

2 tbsp caster sugar

6 tbsp self-raising flour, sifted

125 g/4½ oz desiccated coconut

50 g/1¾ oz plain chocolate,
 optional

1 Grease a shallow 20-cm/8-inch
square cake tin and line the base.

2 Crush the biscuits in a polythene
bag with a rolling pin or process
them in a food processor.

3 Melt the butter or margarine in a
saucepan and stir in the crushed
biscuits until well combined.

4 Press the mixture into the base
of the cake tin.

5 Beat the evaporated milk, egg,
vanilla essence and sugar
together until smooth. Stir in the flour
and desiccated coconut. Pour the
mixture over the biscuit base and
smooth the top.

6 Bake in a preheated oven,
190°C/375°F/Gas Mark 5, for
30 minutes or until the coconut
topping is firm and just golden.

7 Leave the cooked mixture to
cool in the cake tin for about
5 minutes, then cut into squares.
Leave to cool completely in the tin.

8 Carefully remove the squares
from the tin and place them on
a board. Melt the plain chocolate (if
using) and drizzle it over the squares
to decorate them. Leave the chocolate
to set before serving.

VARIATION

Store the squares in an airtight
tin for up to 4 days. They can
be frozen, undecorated, for up
to 2 months. Thaw at
room temperature.

chocolate éclairs

makes ten

CHOUX PASTRY

150 ml/5 fl oz water

70 g/2½ oz butter, cut into
    small pieces

90 g/3 oz strong plain flour, sifted

2 eggs

CRÈME PÂTISSIÈRE

2 eggs, beaten lightly

4 tbsp caster sugar

2 tbsp cornflour

300 ml/10 fl oz milk

¼ tsp vanilla essence

ICING

25 g/1 oz butter

1 tbsp milk

1 tbsp cocoa powder

100 g/3½ oz icing sugar

a little white chocolate, melted

1 Lightly grease a baking tray. Place the water in a saucepan, add the butter and heat gently until the butter melts. Bring to a rolling boil, then remove the pan from the heat and add the flour in one go, beating well until the mixture leaves the sides of the saucepan and forms a ball. Leave to cool slightly, then gradually beat in the eggs to form a smooth, glossy mixture. Spoon into a large piping bag fitted with a 1-cm/½-inch plain nozzle.

2 Sprinkle the baking tray with a little water. Pipe éclairs 7.5 cm/ 3 inches long, spaced well apart. Bake in a preheated oven, 200°C/400°F/Gas Mark 6, for 30–35 minutes or until crisp and golden. Make a small slit in each one to let the steam escape. Cool on a wire rack.

3 Meanwhile, make the crème pâtissière. Whisk the eggs and sugar until thick and creamy, then fold in the cornflour. Heat the milk until almost boiling and pour on to the eggs, whisking. Transfer to the saucepan and cook over a low heat, stirring until thick. Remove from the heat and stir in the vanilla essence. Cover with baking paper and cool.

4 To make the icing, melt the butter with the milk in a saucepan, remove from the heat and stir in the cocoa powder and sugar. Split the éclairs lengthways and pipe in the crème pâtissière. Spread the icing over the top of the éclairs. Spoon over the white chocolate, swirl in and leave to set. If preferred, the éclairs can be filled with whipped cream.

chocolate chip muffins

makes twelve

100 g/3½ oz soft margarine

225 g/8 oz caster sugar

2 large eggs

150 ml/5 fl oz whole-milk natural
   yogurt

5 tbsp milk

275 g/9½ oz plain flour

1 tsp bicarbonate of soda

175 g/6 oz plain chocolate chips

1 Line a 12-muffin tin with paper cases.

2 Place the margarine and sugar in a mixing bowl and beat with a wooden spoon until light and fluffy. Beat in the eggs, yogurt and milk until well combined.

3 Sift the flour and bicarbonate of soda together and add to the mixture. Stir until just blended.

VARIATION

The mixture can also be used to make 6 large or 24 mini muffins. Bake mini muffins for 10 minutes or until springy to the touch.

4 Stir in the chocolate chips, then spoon the mixture into the paper cases and bake in a preheated oven, 190°C/375°F/Gas Mark 5, for 25 minutes or until a fine skewer inserted into the centre comes out clean. Leave to cool in the tin for 5 minutes, then turn out on to a wire rack to cool.

chocolate biscotti

makes sixteen

1 egg

100 g/3½ oz caster sugar

1 tsp vanilla essence

125 g/4½ oz plain flour

½ tsp baking powder

1 tsp ground cinnamon

50 g/1¾ oz plain chocolate,
   chopped roughly

50 g/1¾ oz flaked almonds, toasted

50 g/1¾ oz pine kernels

1 Lightly grease a large baking tray with a little butter. Set aside while you prepare the biscuit mixture.

2 Whisk the egg, sugar and vanilla essence in a mixing bowl with an electric mixer until it is thick and pale – ribbons of mixture should trail from the whisk as you lift it.

3 Sift the flour, baking powder and cinnamon into a separate bowl, then sift into the egg mixture and fold in gently. Stir in the roughly chopped plain chocolate, toasted flaked almonds and pine kernels.

4 Turn out on to a lightly floured work surface and shape into a flat log, 23-cm/9-inches long and 2-cm/¾-inch wide. Transfer to the baking tray.

5 Bake in a preheated oven, 180°C/350°F/Gas Mark 4, for 20–25 minutes or until golden. Remove from the oven and leave to cool for 5 minutes or until firm.

6 Transfer the log to a chopping board. Using a serrated bread knife, cut the log on the diagonal into slices about 1-cm/½-inch thick and arrange them on the baking tray. Cook for 10–15 minutes, turning halfway through the cooking time.

7 Cool for 5 minutes. Transfer to a wire rack to cool completely.

chocolate chip tartlets

serves six

50 g/1¾ oz toasted hazelnuts

150 g/5½ oz plain flour

1 tbsp icing sugar

140 g/5 oz soft margarine

FILLING

2 tbsp cornflour

1 tbsp cocoa powder

1 tbsp caster sugar

300 ml/10 fl oz semi-skimmed milk

3 tbsp chocolate hazelnut spread

2½ tbsp plain chocolate chips

2½ tbsp milk chocolate chips

2½ tbsp white chocolate chips

1 Finely chop the nuts in a food processor. Add the flour, the icing sugar and margarine. Process for a few seconds until the mixture resembles breadcrumbs. Add 2–3 tablespoons of water and process to form a soft dough. Cover and chill in the freezer for 10 minutes.

2 Roll out the dough and use to line 6 loose-bottomed 10-cm/ 4-inch tartlet tins. Prick the bases with a fork and line them with loosely crumpled foil. Bake in a preheated oven, 200°C/400°F/Gas Mark 6, for 15 minutes. Remove the foil and bake for a further 5 minutes, until the pastry cases are crisp and golden. Remove from the oven and leave to cool.

3 Meanwhile make the filling. Mix together the cornflour, cocoa powder and sugar with enough milk to make a smooth paste. Stir in the remaining milk. Pour into a saucepan and cook gently over a low heat, stirring until thickened. Stir in the chocolate hazelnut spread.

4 Mix the chocolate chips together and reserve a quarter. Stir half of the remaining chips into the custard. Cover with damp greaseproof paper and leave until almost cold, then stir in the second half of the chocolate chips. Spoon the mixture into the pastry cases and leave to cool. Scatter the reserved chocolate chips over the top.

chocolate orange biscuits

makes thirty

85 g/3 oz butter, softened

6 tbsp caster sugar

1 egg

1 tbsp milk

225 g/8 oz plain flour

2 tbsp cocoa powder

ICING

175 g/6 oz icing sugar, sifted

3 tbsp orange juice

a little plain chocolate, melted

1 Line 2 baking trays with sheets of baking paper.

2 Beat the butter and sugar together until light and fluffy. Beat in the egg and milk until well combined. Sift the flour and cocoa powder together and gradually mix together to form a soft dough. Use your fingers to incorporate the last of the flour and bring the dough together.

3 Roll out the dough on to a lightly floured work surface until 5-mm/¼-inch thick. Using a 5-cm/2-inch fluted round cutter, cut out as many biscuits as you can. Re-roll the dough trimmings and cut out more biscuits.

4 Place the biscuits on the prepared baking tray and bake in a preheated oven, 180°C/350°F/ Gas Mark 4, for 10–12 minutes or until the biscuits are golden.

5 Leave to cool on the baking tray for a few minutes, then transfer to a wire rack to cool completely.

6 To make the icing, place the icing sugar in a bowl and stir in enough orange juice to form a thin icing that will coat the back of a spoon. Spread the icing over the biscuits and leave to set. Drizzle with melted chocolate. Leave the chocolate to set before serving.

chocolate caramel squares

makes sixteen

100 g/3½ oz soft margarine

4 tbsp light muscovado sugar

125 g/4½ oz plain flour

40 g/1½ oz rolled oats

CARAMEL FILLING

25 g/1 oz butter

2 tbsp light muscovado sugar

200 g/7 oz canned condensed milk

TOPPING

100 g/3½ oz plain chocolate

25 g/1 oz white chocolate, optional

1 Beat the margarine and muscovado sugar together in a bowl until light and fluffy. Beat in the flour and the rolled oats. Use your fingertips to bring the mixture together if necessary.

2 Using your hands, press the mixture into the base of a shallow 20-cm/8-inch square cake tin.

3 Bake in a preheated oven, 180°C/350°F/Gas Mark 4, for 25 minutes or until just golden and firm. Cool the cooked mixture in the tin.

4 Place the ingredients for the caramel filling in a saucepan and heat gently, stirring until the sugar has dissolved and the ingredients combine. Bring slowly to the boil over a very low heat, then boil very gently for 3–4 minutes, stirring constantly, until the filling has thickened.

5 Pour the caramel filling over the biscuit base in the tin, smooth with a palette knife and leave to set.

6 Melt the plain chocolate and spread it over the caramel. If using the white chocolate, melt it and pipe lines of white chocolate over the plain chocolate. Using a cocktail stick or a skewer, feather the white chocolate into the plain chocolate. Leave to set. Cut into squares to serve.

COOK'S TIP

If liked, you can line the tin with baking paper so that the biscuit can be lifted out before cutting into pieces.

malted chocolate wedges

makes sixteen

100 g/3½ oz butter

2 tbsp golden syrup

2 tbsp malted chocolate drink

225 g/8 oz malted milk biscuits

75 g/2¾ oz milk or plain chocolate, broken into pieces

2 tbsp icing sugar

2 tbsp milk

1 Grease a shallow 18-cm/7-inch round cake tin or flan tin and line the base with baking paper.

2 Place the butter, golden syrup and malted chocolate drink in a small saucepan and heat gently, stirring until the butter has melted and the mixture is well combined.

3 Crush the biscuits in a polythene bag with a rolling pin, or process them in a food processor until they form crumbs. Stir the crumbs into the chocolate mixture and mix well.

4 Press the mixture into the prepared tin and then chill in the refrigerator until firm.

5 Place the chocolate pieces in a small heatproof bowl with the icing sugar and the milk. Place the bowl over a saucepan of gently simmering water and stir until the chocolate melts and the mixture is thoroughly combined.

6 Spread the chocolate icing smoothly and evenly over the biscuit base and leave to set in the tin. Using a sharp knife, cut the finished biscuits into wedges to serve.

VARIATION

Add chopped pecan nuts to the biscuit crumb mixture in Step 3, if liked.

chequerboard cookies

makes eighteen

175 g/6 oz butter, softened

6 tbsp icing sugar

1 teaspoon vanilla essence or
    grated rind of ½ orange

250 g/9 oz plain flour

25 g/1 oz plain chocolate, melted

a little beaten egg white

1 Lightly grease a baking tray. Beat the butter and icing sugar in a mixing bowl until they are light and fluffy. Beat in the vanilla essence or the grated orange rind.

2 Gradually beat in the flour to form a soft dough. Use your fingers to incorporate the last of the flour and to bring the dough together.

3 Divide the dough in half and beat the melted chocolate into one half. Keep each half of the dough separate, cover and leave to chill for about 30 minutes.

4 Roll out each piece of dough to a rectangle 7.5 x 20 cm/3 x 8 inches long and 3-cm/1½-inches thick. Brush one piece of dough with a little egg white and place the other on top.

5 Cut the block of dough in half lengthways and turn over one half. Brush the side of one strip with egg white and butt the other up to it, so that it resembles a chequerboard.

6 Cut the block into thin slices and place each slice flat on the baking tray, allowing enough room between them for them to spread out a little during cooking.

7 Bake in a preheated oven, 180°C/350°F/Gas Mark 4, for about 10 minutes, until just firm. Leave to cool on the baking trays for a few minutes, before carefully transferring to a wire rack with a spatula. Leave to cool completely.

chocolate meringues

makes eight

4 egg whites

225 g/8 oz caster sugar

1 tsp cornflour

40 g/1½ oz plain chocolate, grated

TO COMPLETE

100 g/3½ oz plain chocolate

150 ml/5 fl oz double cream

1 tbsp icing sugar

1 tbsp brandy, optional

1 Line 2 baking trays with baking paper. Whisk the egg whites until standing in soft peaks, then gradually whisk in half of the sugar. Continue whisking until the meringue mixture is very stiff and glossy.

2 Carefully fold the remaining sugar, cornflour and grated chocolate into the meringue mixture with a metal spoon or spatula.

3 Spoon the mixture into a piping bag fitted with a large star or plain nozzle. Pipe 16 large rosettes or mounds on the lined baking trays.

4 Bake in a preheated oven, 140°C/275°F/Gas Mark 1, for about 1 hour, changing the position of the baking trays halfway through cooking. Without opening the oven door, turn off the oven and leave the meringues to cool in the oven. Once cold, carefully peel away the baking paper.

5 Melt the plain chocolate and spread it over the base of the meringues. Stand them upside down on a wire rack until the chocolate has set. Whip the cream, icing sugar and

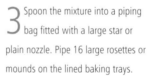

brandy (if using) until the cream holds its shape. Spoon into a piping bag and use to sandwich the meringues together in pairs. Serve.

VARIATION

To make mini meringues, use a star-shaped nozzle and pipe about 24 small rosettes. Bake for about 40 minutes until crisp.

mexican chocolate meringues

makes twenty-five

4–5 egg whites, at room
    temperature

pinch of salt

¼ tsp cream of tartar

¼–½ tsp vanilla essence

175–200 g/6–7 oz caster sugar

⅛–¼ tsp ground cinnamon

115 g/4 oz continental plain or plain
    chocolate, grated

TO SERVE

ground cinnamon, for dusting

115 g/4 oz strawberries

chocolate-flavoured cream (see
    Cook's Tip)

1 Whisk the egg whites until they are foamy, then add the salt and cream of tartar and beat until very stiff. Whisk in the vanilla essence, then slowly whisk in the sugar, a small amount at a time, until the meringue is shiny and stiff. This should take about 3 minutes by hand, and less than a minute if you use an electric mixer.

2 Whisk in the cinnamon and grated chocolate. Spoon mounds of about 2 tablespoons on to an ungreased, non-stick baking sheet. Space the mounds well apart.

3 Place in a preheated oven at 150°C/300°F/Gas Mark 2 and cook for 2 hours until set.

4 Remove from the baking sheet. If the meringues are too moist and soft, return them to the oven to firm up and dry out more. Cool.

COOK'S TIP

To make the flavoured cream, simply stir half-melted chocolate pieces into stiffly whipped cream, then chill until solid.

5 Serve the meringues dusted with cinnamon and accompanied by strawberries and a little chocolate-flavoured whipped cream.

viennese chocolate fingers

makes eighteen

125 g/4½ oz unsalted butter

6 tbsp icing sugar

175 g/6 oz self-raising flour, sifted

3 tbsp cornflour

200 g/7 oz plain chocolate

1 Lightly grease 2 baking trays. Beat the butter and sugar in a mixing bowl until light and fluffy. Gradually beat in the flour and cornflour.

2 Melt 75 g/2¾ oz of the plain chocolate and beat into the biscuit dough.

3 Place the mixture in a piping bag fitted with a large star nozzle and pipe fingers, 5 cm/2 inches long on the baking trays, spaced apart to allow the biscuits to spread during cooking.

4 Bake in a preheated oven, 190°C/375°F/Gas Mark 5, for 12–15 minutes.

COOK'S TIP

If the biscuit dough is too thick to pipe, beat in a little milk to thin it out a little before you place it in the piping bag.

5 Leave the biscuits to cool slightly on the baking trays, then transfer with a spatula to a wire rack and leave to cool completely.

6 Melt the remaining chocolate and dip one end of each biscuit in the chocolate, allowing the excess to drip back into the bowl.

7 Place the chocolate-dipped biscuits on a sheet of baking paper and leave to set before serving.

chocolate hazelnut palmiers

makes twenty-six

TOPPING

375 g/13 oz ready-made puff pastry

8 tbsp chocolate hazelnut spread

50 g/1¾ oz chopped toasted
   hazelnuts

2 tbsp caster sugar

1 Lightly grease a baking tray. Roll out the puff pastry on a lightly floured work surface to a rectangle about 38 x 23 cm/15 x 9 inches.

2 Spread the chocolate hazelnut spread over the pastry using a palette knife, then scatter the chopped hazelnuts over the top.

3 Roll up one long side of the pastry to the centre, then roll up the other side so that they meet in the centre. Where the pieces meet, dampen the edges with a little water to join them. Using a sharp knife, cut into thin slices. Place each slice on to the prepared baking tray and flatten slightly with a palette knife. Sprinkle the slices with the caster sugar.

VARIATION

For an extra chocolate flavour, dip the palmiers in melted plain chocolate to half-cover each biscuit. Place the chocolate-dipped palmiers on a sheet of baking paper and leave them to set.

4 Bake in a preheated oven, 220°C/425°F/Gas Mark 7, for about 10–15 minutes, until golden. Transfer to a wire rack to cool.

rice pudding tartlets

serves six

1 packet frozen shortcrust pastry

1 litre/1¾ pints milk

pinch of salt

100 g/3½ oz arborio or short-grain
    white rice

1 vanilla pod, split, seeds removed
    and reserved

1 tbsp cornflour

2 tbsp sugar

cocoa powder, for dusting

melted chocolate, to decorate

CHOCOLATE GANACHE

200 ml/7 fl oz double cream

1 tbsp golden syrup

175 g/6 oz continental plain or plain
    chocolate, chopped

15 g/½ oz unsalted butter

1 Thaw the pastry, and then use it to line six 10-cm/4-inch tartlet tins. Fill them with baking beans and bake blind in a preheated oven, to 200°C/400°F/Gas Mark 6 for about 20 minutes, until the pastry is set and golden at the edges. Transfer to a wire rack to cool.

2 To make the ganache, bring the cream and golden syrup to the boil. Remove from the heat and immediately stir in the chopped chocolate. Stir until melted and smooth. Beat in the butter. Spoon a 2.5-cm/1-inch thick layer into each tartlet. Set aside.

3 Bring the milk and salt to the boil in a saucepan. Sprinkle in the rice and return to the boil. Add the vanilla seeds and pod. Reduce the heat and simmer gently until the rice is tender and the milk creamy.

4 Blend the cornflour and sugar in a small bowl and add about 2 tablespoons of water to make a paste. Stir in a few spoonfuls of the rice mixture, then stir the cornflour mixture into the rice. Bring to the boil and cook for about 1 minute, until thickened. Cool the saucepan in iced water, stirring until thick.

5 Spoon the rice mixture into the tartlets, filling each to the brim. Leave to set at room temperature. To serve the rice pudding tartlets, dust lightly with cocoa powder and pipe or drizzle a little melted chocolate over each.

chocolate brownies

makes twelve

55 g/2 oz unsweetened stoned
  dates, chopped

55 g/2 oz no-soak prunes, chopped

6 tbsp unsweetened apple juice

4 medium eggs, beaten

300 g/10½ oz dark muscovado
  sugar

1 tsp vanilla essence

4 tbsp low-fat drinking chocolate
  powder, plus extra for dusting

2 tbsp cocoa powder

175 g/6 oz plain flour

55 g/2 oz plain chocolate chips

ICING

125 g/4½ oz icing sugar

1–2 tsp water

1 tsp vanilla essence

COOK'S TIP

Make double the amount,
cut one of the cakes into bars
and open-freeze, then store in
polythene bags. Take out pieces
of cake as and when you need
them – they'll take no time
at all to thaw.

1 Preheat the oven to 180°C/
350°F/Gas Mark 4. Grease and
line an 18 x 28-cm/7 x 11-inch cake tin
with baking paper. Place the dates and
prunes in a small saucepan and add
the apple juice. Bring to the boil, cover
and simmer for 10 minutes until soft.
Beat the mixture to form a smooth
paste, then leave to cool.

2 Place the cooled fruit mixture in a
large bowl and stir in the eggs,
sugar and vanilla essence. Sift in 4
tablespoons of the drinking chocolate,
the cocoa powder and flour, and fold in
together with the chocolate chips until
well combined.

3 Spoon the mixture into the
prepared tin and smooth over the
top. Bake for 25–30 minutes, until firm
to the touch or until a skewer inserted
into the centre comes out clean. Cut
into 12 bars and leave to cool in the tin
for 10 minutes. Transfer to a wire rack
to cool completely.

4 To make the icing, sift the icing
sugar into a bowl and mix with
enough water and the vanilla essence
to form a soft, but not too runny, icing.

5 Drizzle the icing over the brownies
and leave to set. Dust with the
extra chocolate powder before serving.

206

cannoli

makes twenty

3 tbsp lemon juice

3 tbsp water

1 large egg

250 g/9 oz plain flour

1 tbsp caster sugar

1 tsp ground mixed spice

pinch of salt

25 g/1 oz butter, softened

sunflower oil, for deep-frying

1 small egg white, beaten lightly

icing sugar

FILLING

750 g/1 lb 10 oz ricotta cheese, drained

4 tbsp icing sugar

1 tsp vanilla essence

finely grated rind of 1 large orange

4 tbsp very finely chopped candied peel

50 g/1¾ oz plain chocolate, grated

pinch of ground cinnamon

2 tbsp Marsala wine or orange juice

1 Combine the lemon juice, water and egg. Put the flour, sugar, spice and salt into a food processor and quickly process. Add the butter, then with the motor running, pour the egg mixture through the feed tube. Process until the mixture just forms a dough.

2 Turn the dough out on to a lightly floured surface and knead lightly. Wrap and chill for at least 1 hour.

3 Meanwhile, make the filling. Beat the ricotta cheese until smooth. Sift in the icing sugar, then beat in the remaining ingredients. Cover with clingfilm and chill until required.

4 Roll out the dough on a floured surface until 2 mm/¹⁄₁₆-inch thick. Using a ruler, cut out 8.5 x 7.5-cm/3 ½ x 3-inch pieces, re-rolling and cutting the trimmings, making about 20 pieces in all.

5 Heat 5 cm/2 inches of oil in a deep, heavy-based frying pan to 190°C/375°F. Roll a piece of pastry around a greased cannoli mould, to just overlap the edge. Seal with egg white, pressing firmly. Repeat with all the moulds you have. Deep-fry 2 or 3 moulds until the cannoli are golden, crisp and bubbly.

6 Remove the cannoli with a slotted spoon and drain on kitchen paper. Leave until cool, then carefully slide them off the moulds. Repeat with the remaining cannoli.

7 Store unfilled in an airtight container for up to 2 days. Pipe in the filling no more than 30 minutes before serving to prevent the pastry becoming soggy. Sift icing sugar over the cannoli and serve.

chocolate & coconut cookies

makes twenty-four

125 g/4½ oz soft margarine

1 tsp vanilla essence

85 g/3 oz icing sugar, sifted

125 g/4½ oz plain flour

2 tbsp cocoa powder

50 g/1¾ oz desiccated coconut

25 g/1 oz butter

100 g/3½ oz white marshmallows

25 g/1 oz desiccated coconut

a little white chocolate, grated

1 Lightly grease a baking tray. Beat the margarine, vanilla essence and icing sugar together in a mixing bowl until fluffy. Sift the flour and cocoa powder together and beat it into the mixture with the coconut.

2 Roll teaspoons of the mixture into balls and place on the baking tray. Allow room for them to spread out during cooking.

3 Flatten the rounds slightly and bake in a preheated oven, 180°C/350°F/Gas Mark 4, for about 12–15 minutes, until just firm. Remove from the oven.

4 Leave the chocolate and coconut cookies to cool on the baking tray for a few minutes before transferring to a wire rack. Leave the cookies to cool completely.

5 To make the icing, place the butter and white marshmallows in a small saucepan and heat gently, stirring until melted. Spread a little of the marshmallow icing mixture over each biscuit, using a knife or small spoon, and dip in the dessicated coconut. Leave to set. Decorate the chocolate and coconut cookies with a little grated white chocolate before serving.

dutch macaroons

makes twenty

rice paper

2 egg whites

225 g/8 oz caster sugar

175 g/6 oz ground almonds

225 g/8 oz plain chocolate

1 Cover 2 baking trays with rice paper. Whisk the egg whites in a large mixing bowl until stiff, then fold in the sugar and ground almonds.

2 Place the mixture in a large piping bag fitted with a 1-cm/½-inch plain nozzle and pipe fingers, about 7.5 cm/3 inches long, allowing space between them for the mixture to spread out during cooking.

3 Bake the macaroons in a preheated oven, 180°C/350°F/ Gas Mark 4, for 15–20 minutes, until golden. Transfer to a wire rack and leave to cool. Remove the excess rice paper from around the edges.

4 Melt the chocolate and dip the base of each biscuit into the chocolate. Place the macaroons on a sheet of baking paper and leave to set.

COOK'S TIP

Rice paper is edible so you can just break off the excess from around the edge of the biscuits. Remove it completely before dipping in the chocolate, if you prefer.

5 Drizzle any remaining melted chocolate over the top of the biscuits (you may have to re-heat the chocolate in order to do this). Leave to set before serving.

chocolate chip flapjacks

makes twelve

125 g/4½ oz butter

75 g/2¾ oz caster sugar

1 tbsp golden syrup

350 g/12 oz rolled oats

75 g/2¾ oz plain chocolate chips

50 g/1¾ oz sultanas

COOK'S TIP

The flapjacks will keep in an airtight container for up to 1 week, but they are so delicious they are unlikely to last that long!

1 Lightly grease a shallow 20-cm/ 8-inch square cake tin.

2 Place the butter, caster sugar and golden syrup in a saucepan and cook over a low heat, stirring until the butter and sugar melt and the mixture is thoroughly combined.

3 Remove the pan from the heat and stir in the rolled oats until they are well coated. Add the chocolate chips and the sultanas and mix well.

4 Turn into the prepared tin and press down well.

5 Bake in a preheated oven, 180°C/350°F/Gas Mark 4, for 30 minutes. Cool slightly, then mark into fingers. When almost cold, cut into bars or squares and transfer to a wire rack until cold.

chocolate chip cookies

makes eighteen

175 g/6 oz plain flour

1 tsp baking powder

125 g/4½ oz soft margarine

85 g/3 oz light muscovado sugar

5 tbsp caster sugar

½ tsp vanilla essence

1 egg

125 g/4½ oz plain chocolate chips

VARIATION

For Choc & Nut Cookies, add 40 g/1½ oz chopped hazelnuts to the basic mixture.
For Double Choc Cookies, beat in 40 g/1½ oz melted plain chocolate.
For White Chocolate Chip Cookies, use white chocolate chips instead of the plain chocolate chips.

1 Place all of the ingredients in a large mixing bowl and beat until they are well combined.

2 Lightly grease 2 baking trays. Place tablespoonfuls of the chocolate chip mixture on to the baking trays, spacing them well apart to allow for spreading during cooking.

3 Bake in a preheated oven, 190°C/375°F/Gas Mark 5, for 10–12 minutes or until the cookies are golden brown.

4 Using a palette knife, carefully transfer the chocolate chip cookies to a wire rack and let them cool completely.

millionaire's shortbread

serves four

175 g/6 oz plain flour

125 g/4½ oz butter, cut into small
  pieces

4 tbsp soft brown sugar, sifted

TOPPING

55 g/2 oz butter

4 tbsp soft brown sugar

400 g/14 oz canned condensed milk

150 g/5½ oz milk chocolate

1 Grease a 23-cm/9-inch square
cake tin with butter.

2 Sift the flour into a mixing bowl
and rub in the butter with your
fingertips until the mixture resembles
fine breadcrumbs. Add the sugar and
mix to form a firm dough.

3 Press the dough into the base of
the prepared tin and prick all over
with a fork.

4 Bake in a preheated oven,
190°C/375°F/Gas Mark 5, for
20 minutes, until lightly golden. Leave
the shortbread to cool in the tin.

5 To make the topping, place the
butter, sugar and condensed milk
in a non-stick saucepan and cook over
a gentle heat, stirring constantly, until
the mixture comes to the boil.

COOK'S TIP

Ensure the caramel layer
is completely cool and set
before coating it with the
melted chocolate, otherwise
they will mix together.

6 Reduce the heat and cook for
4–5 minutes, until the caramel is
pale golden and thick and is coming
away from the sides of the pan. Pour
the topping over the shortbread base
and leave to cool.

7 When the caramel topping is
firm, melt the milk chocolate in a
heatproof bowl set over a saucepan
of simmering water. Spread the melted
chocolate over the topping, leave to
set in a cool place, then cut the
shortbread into squares or fingers.

florentines

makes ten

55 g/2 oz butter

4 tbsp caster sugar

3 tbsp plain flour, sifted

50 g/1¾ oz almonds, chopped

50 g/1¾ oz chopped mixed peel

25 g/1 oz raisins, chopped

25 g/1 oz glacé cherries, chopped

finely grated rind of ½ lemon

125 g/4½ oz plain chocolate, melted

VARIATION

Replace the plain chocolate with white chocolate or, for a dramatic effect, cover half of the florentines in plain chocolate and half in white.

---

1 Line 2 large baking trays with baking paper. Set aside.

2 Heat the butter and caster sugar together in a small saucepan until the butter has just melted and the sugar dissolved. Remove the saucepan from the heat.

3 Stir in the flour and mix well. Stir in the chopped almonds, mixed peel, raisins, cherries and lemon rind. Place teaspoonfuls of the mixture well apart on the baking trays.

4 Bake in a preheated oven, 180°C/350°F/Gas Mark 4, for 10 minutes or until lightly golden.

5 As soon as the florentines are removed from the oven, press the edges into neat shapes whilst still on the baking trays, using a biscuit cutter. Leave the florentines to cool on the baking trays until firm, then transfer to a wire rack to cool completely.

6 Spread the melted chocolate over the smooth side of each florentine. As the chocolate begins to set, mark wavy lines in it with a fork. Leave the florentines until set, chocolate-side up.

lemon chocolate pinwheels

makes forty

175 g/6 oz butter, softened

300 g/10½ oz caster sugar

1 egg, beaten

350 g/12 oz plain flour

25 g/1 oz plain chocolate, melted
  and cooled slightly

grated rind of 1 lemon

COOK'S TIP

To make rolling out easier, place
each piece of dough between
2 sheets of baking paper.

1 Grease and flour several baking
trays, enough to accommodate
40 biscuits comfortably.

2 Cream the butter and sugar in a
large mixing bowl until light
and fluffy.

3 Gradually add the beaten egg to
the creamed mixture, beating well
after each addition.

4 Sift the flour into the creamed
mixture and mix thoroughly until a
soft dough forms.

5 Transfer half of the dough to
another bowl and then beat in the
cooled melted chocolate until
thoroughly combined.

6 Stir the grated lemon rind into the
other half of the plain dough.

7 Roll out the 2 pieces of dough
on a lightly floured work surface
to form rectangles of the same size.

8 Lay the lemon dough on top of
the chocolate dough. Roll up the
dough tightly into a sausage shape,
using a sheet of baking paper to guide
you. Leave the dough to chill in the
refrigerator to firm up.

9 Cut the roll into about 40 slices,
place them on the baking trays
and bake in a preheated oven,
190°C/375°F/Gas Mark 5, for
10–12 minutes or until lightly golden.
Transfer the lemon chocolate
pinwheels to a wire rack and leave
to cool completely before serving.

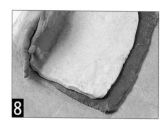

chocolate pretzels

makes thirty

100 g/3½ oz unsalted butter

100 g/3½ oz caster sugar

1 egg

225 g/8 oz plain flour

2 tbsp cocoa powder

TO FINISH

15 g/½ oz butter

100 g/3½ oz plain chocolate

icing sugar, for dusting

1 Lightly grease a baking tray with a little butter. Beat together the butter and sugar in a large mixing bowl until light and fluffy. Beat in the egg, ensuring all the ingredients are well combined.

2 Sift the flour and cocoa powder together and gradually beat into the egg mixture to form a soft dough. Use your fingers to incorporate the last of the flour and bring the dough together. Chill for 15 minutes.

3 Break pieces from the dough and roll into thin sausage shapes about 10 cm/4 inches long and 5-mm/¼-inch thick. Carefully twist into pretzel shapes by making a circle, then twist the ends through each other to form a letter 'B'.

4 Place the chocolate pretzels on the prepared baking tray, slightly spaced apart to allow for spreading during cooking.

5 Bake in a preheated oven, 190°C/375°F/Gas Mark 5, for 8–12 minutes. Leave the pretzels to cool slightly on the baking tray, then transfer to a wire rack to cool completely.

6 Melt the butter and chocolate in a bowl set over a saucepan of gently simmering water, stirring.

7 Dip half of each pretzel into the chocolate and allow the excess chocolate to drip back into the bowl. Place the pretzels on a sheet of baking paper and leave to set.

8 When set, dust the non-chocolate coated side of each pretzel with icing sugar before serving.

220

chocolate boxes

serves six

225 g/8 oz plain chocolate

about 225 g/8 oz bought or ready-
made plain or chocolate cake

2 tbsp apricot jam

150 ml/5 fl oz double cream

1 tbsp maple syrup

100 g/3½ oz prepared fresh fruit,
such as small strawberries,
raspberries, kiwi fruit or
redcurrants

1 Melt the plain chocolate and
spread it evenly over a large
sheet of baking paper. Leave to
harden in a cool room.

2 When just set, cut the chocolate
into 5-cm/2-inch squares and
remove from the baking paper. Make
sure that your hands are as cool as
possible and handle the chocolate as
little as possible.

3 Cut the cake into two 5-cm/2-inch
cubes, then cut each cube in half.
Warm the apricot jam in a small
saucepan and brush it evenly over
the sides of the cake cubes. Carefully
press a chocolate square on to each
side of the cake cubes to make
4 chocolate boxes with cake at the
bottom. Leave to chill in the
refrigerator for 20 minutes.

4 Whip the cream with the maple
syrup until just holding its shape.
Spoon or pipe a little of the mixture
into each chocolate box.

5 Decorate the top of each box with
the prepared fruit. If liked, the fruit
can be partially dipped into melted
chocolate and allowed to harden
before being placed into the boxes.

fried chocolate fingers

makes twenty-four

4 eggs, beaten lightly

600 ml/1 pint milk

5 tbsp sherry

8 x 1-cm/½-inch thick slices of day-
old white bread

4 tbsp sunflower oil

115 g/4 oz caster sugar

225 g/8 oz plain chocolate, grated

vanilla ice cream, to serve (optional)

1 Pour the beaten eggs, milk and sherry into a shallow dish and beat lightly to mix. Cut each slice of bread lengthways into 3 fingers. Soak the bread fingers in the egg mixture until soft, then drain them on kitchen paper.

2 Heat the oil in a large, heavy-based frying pan. Carefully add the bread fingers to the pan, in batches, and cook over a medium heat for 12 minutes on each side, until golden. Using tongs, transfer the fingers to kitchen paper to drain.

3 When all the fingers are cooked and thoroughly drained, roll them first in the sugar and then in the grated chocolate. Pile them on a warmed serving plate and serve immediately, with vanilla ice cream if wished.

meringue fingers

makes thirty

1 egg white

4 tbsp caster sugar

1½ tsp cocoa powder

140 g/5 oz plain chocolate, broken

    into pieces

1 Line a baking tray with baking paper. Whisk the egg white until it forms soft peaks. Whisk in half the sugar and continue whisking until stiff and glossy. Fold in the remaining sugar and the cocoa powder.

2 Spoon the mixture into a piping bag fitted with a 1-cm/½-inch round nozzle. Pipe fingers about 7.5-cm/3-inches long on the prepared baking tray, spacing them at least 2.5 cm/1 inch apart. Bake in a preheated oven 120°C/250°F/Gas Mark ½. for 1 hour, until completely dry. Remove from the oven and transfer to a wire rack to cool.

3 Put the chocolate in the top of a double boiler or in a heatproof bowl set over a saucepan of barely simmering water. Heat, stirring constantly, until the chocolate has melted and the mixture is smooth. Remove from the heat. Cool slightly, then dip the meringue fingers into the mixture, one at a time, to half-coat them. You can either coat one end completely, leaving the other plain, or dip the fingers at an angle so half the length is coated. Place the fingers on baking paper to set.

Sweets & Drinks

There is nothing quite as nice as home-made chocolates and sweets – they leave the average box of chocolates in the shade! You'll find recipes in this chapter to suit everybody's taste. Wonderful, rich, melt-in-the-mouth Italian Chocolate Truffles, Chocolate Marzipans, Nutty Chocolate Clusters, Mini Chocolate Tartlets and rich Chocolate Liqueurs – they're all here. There is even some Easy Chocolate Fudge, so there is no need to fiddle about with sugar thermometers.

Looking for something to wash it all down? We have included delightfully cool summer chocolate drinks and, for warmth and comfort on winter nights, hot drinks that will simply put instant hot chocolate to shame. Enjoy!

chocolate liqueurs

makes forty

100 g/3½ oz plain chocolate

about 5 glacé cherries, halved

about 10 hazelnuts or macadamia
    nuts

150 ml/5 fl oz double cream

2 tbsp icing sugar

4 tbsp liqueur

TO FINISH

50 g/1¾ oz plain chocolate, melted

a little white chocolate, melted or
    white chocolate quick curls
    (see page 7) or extra nuts and
    cherries

COOK'S TIP

Sweet cases can vary in size.
Use the smallest you can find
for this recipe.

---

1 Line a baking tray with a sheet of baking paper. Break the chocolate into pieces, place in a bowl and set over a saucepan of hot water. Stir until melted. Spoon into 20 paper sweet cases, spreading up the sides with a small spoon or pastry brush. Place upside down on the prepared baking tray and leave to set.

2 Carefully peel away the paper cases. Place a cherry or nut in the base of each cup.

3 To make the filling, place the cream in a bowl and sift the icing sugar on top. Whip the cream until it is just holding its shape, then whisk in the liqueur.

4 Place the cream in a piping bag fitted with a 1-cm/½-inch plain nozzle and pipe a little into each chocolate case. Leave to chill for 20 minutes.

5 To finish, spoon the melted plain chocolate over the cream to cover it and pipe the melted white chocolate on top, swirling it into the plain

chocolate with a cocktail stick. Leave the chocolates to harden. Alternatively, cover the cream with the melted plain chocolate and decorate with white chocolate curls before setting. Or, if you prefer, place a small piece of nut or cherry on top of the cream and then cover with plain chocolate.

nutty chocolate clusters

makes thirty

175 g/6 oz white chocolate

100 g/3½ oz digestive biscuits

100 g/3½ oz macadamia nuts or
brazil nuts, chopped

25 g/1 oz stem ginger, chopped
(optional)

175 g/6 oz plain chocolate

1 Line a baking tray with baking paper. Break the white chocolate into small pieces and place in a large mixing bowl set over a saucepan of gently simmering water. Stir until melted.

2 Break the digestive biscuits into small pieces. Stir the biscuits into the melted chocolate with the chopped nuts and stem ginger (if using).

3 Carefully place heaped teaspoons of the mixture on to the prepared baking tray.

4 Chill the chocolate cluster mixture until set, then carefully remove from the baking paper.

5 Melt the chocolate and leave it to cool slightly. Dip the clusters into the melted chocolate, allowing the excess to drip back into the bowl. Return the clusters to the baking tray and chill until set.

fruit & nut fudge

makes twenty-five

250 g/9 oz plain chocolate

25 g/1 oz butter

4 tbsp canned evaporated milk

450 g/1 lb icing sugar, sifted

50 g/1¾ oz roughly chopped
  hazelnuts

50 g/1¾ oz sultanas

VARIATION

Vary the nuts used in this
recipe; try making the fudge
with almonds, brazil nuts,
walnuts or pecan nuts.

1 Lightly grease a 20-cm/8-inch
square cake tin.

2 Break the chocolate into pieces
and place it in a bowl with the
butter and evaporated milk. Set the
bowl over a saucepan of gently
simmering water and stir until the
chocolate and butter have melted and
the ingredients are well combined.

3 Remove the bowl from the heat
and gradually beat in the icing
sugar. Stir the hazelnuts and sultanas
into the mixture. Press the fudge into
the prepared tin and smooth the top.
Leave the fudge to chill in the
refrigerator until firm.

4 Tip the fudge out on to a
chopping board and cut into
squares. Place in paper sweet cases.
Chill until required.

mini chocolate tartlets

makes eighteen

175 g/6 oz plain flour

85 g/3 oz butter

1 tbsp caster sugar

about 1 tbsp water

FILLING

100 g/3½ oz full-fat soft cheese

2 tbsp caster sugar

1 small egg, beaten lightly

50 g/1¾ oz plain chocolate

TO DECORATE

100 ml/10 fl oz double cream

plain chocolate quick curls (see
    page 7)

cocoa powder, for dusting

COOK'S TIP

The tartlets can be made up to 3 days ahead. Decorate on the day of serving, preferably no more than 4 hours in advance.

1 Sift the flour into a mixing bowl. Cut the butter into small pieces and rub in with your fingertips until the mixture resembles fine breadcrumbs. Stir in the sugar. Add enough water to mix to a soft dough, then cover and chill for 15 minutes.

2 Roll out the pastry on a lightly floured surface and use to line 18 mini tartlet tins or mini muffin tins. Prick the bases with a cocktail stick.

3 Beat the full-fat soft cheese and sugar together. Beat in the egg. Melt the chocolate and beat it into the mixture. Spoon into the pastry cases and bake in a preheated oven, 190°C/375°F/Gas Mark 5, for 15 minutes, until the pastry is crisp and the soft cheese and filling set. Place the tins on a wire rack and leave to cool completely.

4 Chill the tartlets in the refrigerator. Whip the double cream until it is just holding its shape. Place the cream in a piping bag fitted with a star nozzle and pipe rosettes of whipped cream on top of the chocolate tartlets. Decorate with chocolate curls and finish with a dusting of cocoa powder.

rocky road bites

makes eighteen

FILLING

125 g/4½ oz milk chocolate

50 g/2½ oz mini multi-coloured
  marshmallows

25 g/1 oz chopped walnuts

25 g/1 oz no-soak apricots,
  chopped

VARIATION

If you cannot find mini
marshmallows, use large ones
and chop them into smaller
pieces with kitchen scissors
before mixing them into the
melted chocolate.

1 Line a baking tray with baking
paper and set aside.

2 Break the milk chocolate into
small pieces and place in a large
mixing bowl. Set the bowl over a
saucepan of simmering water and stir
until the chocolate has melted.

3 Stir in the marshmallows, walnuts
and apricots and toss in the
melted chocolate until well covered.

4 Place heaped teaspoons of
the marshmallow mixture on to
the prepared baking tray.

5 Leave the sweets to chill in
the refrigerator until set.

6 Once set, carefully remove the
sweets from the baking paper.

7 These chewy marshmallow bites
can be placed in paper sweet
cases to serve, if wished.

chocolate mascarpone cups

makes twenty

100 g/3½ oz plain chocolate

FILLING

100 g/3½ oz milk or plain chocolate

200 g/7 oz mascarpone cheese

¼ tsp vanilla essence

cocoa powder, for dusting

VARIATION

Substitute full-fat crème fraîche for marscapone cheese. Its delicate flavour blends well with chocolate.

1 Line a baking tray with a sheet of baking paper. Break 100 g/3½ oz plain chocolate into pieces, place in a bowl and set over a saucepan of hot water. Stir until the chocolate has melted. Spoon the melted chocolate into 20 paper sweet cases, spreading up the sides with a small spoon or pastry brush. Place upside down on the baking tray and leave to set.

2 When set, carefully peel away the paper cases.

3 For the filling, melt the chocolate. Place the mascarpone cheese in a bowl and beat in the vanilla essence and melted chocolate until well combined. Leave the mixture to chill in the refrigerator, beating occasionally, until firm enough to pipe.

4 Place the mascarpone filling in a piping bag fitted with a star nozzle and pipe the mixture into the cups. Decorate the cups with a dusting of cocoa powder.

233

rum truffles

makes twenty

125 g/5½ oz plain chocolate

small knob of butter

2 tbsp rum

50 g/1¾ oz desiccated coconut

100 g/3½ oz cake crumbs

6 tbsp icing sugar

2 tbsp cocoa powder

COOK'S TIP

Make sure the chocolate is cut into even sized pieces. This way you will ensure that it all melts at the same rate.

1 Break the chocolate into pieces and place in a bowl with the butter. Set the bowl over a saucepan of gently simmering water, stir until melted and combined.

2 Remove from the heat and beat in the rum. Stir in the desiccated coconut, cake crumbs and two-thirds of the icing sugar. Beat until combined. Add a little extra rum if the chocolate coconut mixture is too stiff.

3 Roll the mixture into small balls and place them on a sheet of baking paper. Leave to chill until firm.

4 Sift the remaining icing sugar on to a large plate. Sift the cocoa powder on to another plate. Roll half of the truffles in the icing sugar until thoroughly coated and roll the remaining truffles in the cocoa powder.

5 Place the finished rum truffles in paper sweet cases and leave them to chill until required.

VARIATION

Make the truffles with white chocolate and replace the rum with coconut-flavoured liqueur or milk, if you prefer. Roll them in cocoa powder or dip in melted milk chocolate.

mini chocolate cones

makes ten

75 g/2¾ oz plain chocolate

100 ml/3½ fl oz double cream

1 tbsp icing sugar

1 tbsp crème de menthe

chocolate coffee beans, to decorate
(optional)

1 Cut ten 7.5-cm/3-inch circles of baking paper. Carefully shape each circle into a cone shape and secure with sticky tape.

2 Break the chocolate into pieces, place in a bowl and set over a saucepan of hot water. Stir until the chocolate has melted. Using a small pastry brush or clean artist's brush, brush the inside of each cone with the melted plain chocolate.

3 Brush a second layer of chocolate on the inside of the cones and leave to chill until set. Carefully peel away the paper.

4 Place the cream, icing sugar and crème de menthe in a mixing bowl and whip until just holding its shape. Place in a piping bag fitted with a star nozzle and pipe the mixture into the chocolate cones.

5 Decorate the cones with chocolate coffee beans (if using) and chill until required.

collettes

100 g/3½ oz white chocolate
FILLING
150 g/5½ oz orange-flavoured
    plain chocolate
150 ml/5 fl oz double cream
2 tbsp icing sugar

COOK'S TIP

If they do not hold their
shape well, use 2 cases to
make a double thickness mould.
Foil cases are firmer, so use
these if you can find them.

1 Line a baking tray with a sheet of baking paper. Break the chocolate into pieces, place in a bowl and set over a saucepan of hot water. Stir until melted, and spoon into 20 paper sweet cases, spreading up the sides with a small pastry brush. Place upside down on the prepared baking tray and leave to set.

2 When set, carefully peel away the paper cases.

3 To make the filling, melt the orange-flavoured chocolate and place in a mixing bowl with the cream and the icing sugar. Beat the chocolate cream until smooth. Chill until the mixture becomes firm enough to pipe, stirring occasionally.

4 Place the filling in a piping bag fitted with a star nozzle and pipe a little into each case. Leave to chill until required.

chocolate marzipans

makes thirty

450 g/1 lb marzipan

25 g/1 oz glacé cherries, chopped
   very finely

25 g/1 oz stem ginger, chopped
   very finely

50 g/1¾ oz no-soak dried apricots,
   chopped very finely

350 g/12 oz plain chocolate

25 g/1 oz white chocolate

icing sugar, for dusting

1 Line a baking tray with a sheet of baking paper. Divide the marzipan into 3 balls and knead each ball to soften it.

2 Work the glacé cherries into one portion of the marzipan by kneading on a work surface lightly dusted with icing sugar.

3 Do the same with the stem ginger and another portion of marzipan and then the apricots and the third portion of marzipan.

4 Form each flavoured portion of marzipan into small balls, keeping the different flavours separate.

5 Break the plain chocolate into pieces, place in a bowl and set over a pan of hot water. Stir until the chocolate has melted. Dip one of each flavoured ball of marzipan into the melted chocolate by spiking each one with a cocktail stick, allowing the excess chocolate to drip back into the bowl.

6 Place the balls in clusters made up of the 3 flavours on the baking tray. Repeat with the remaining marzipan balls. Chill until set.

7 Melt the white chocolate and drizzle a little over the tops of each cluster of marzipan balls. Chill until hardened, then remove the marzipan balls from the baking paper and dust with sugar to serve.

VARIATION

Coat the marzipan balls in white or milk chocolate and drizzle with plain chocolate, if you prefer.

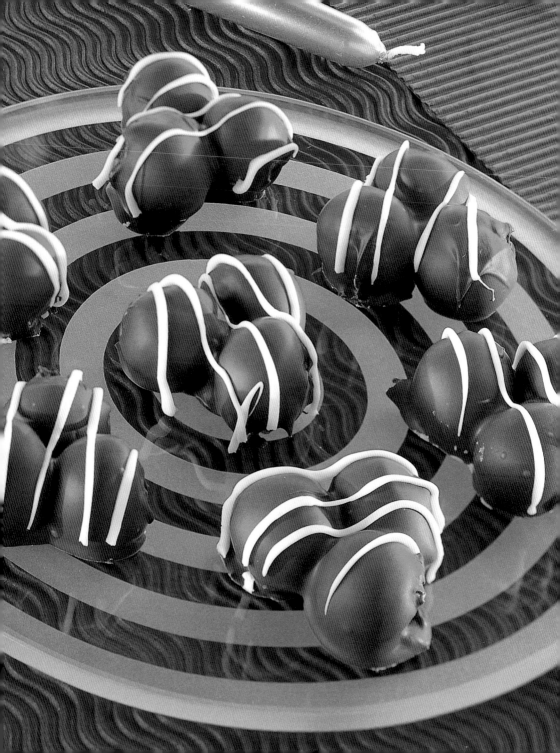

mini florentines

makes forty

85 g/3 oz butter

75 g/2¾ oz caster sugar

2 tbsp sultanas or raisins

2 tbsp glacé cherries, chopped

2 tbsp crystallised ginger, chopped

25 g/1 oz sunflower seeds

100 g/3½ oz flaked almonds

2 tbsp double cream

175 g/6 oz plain or milk chocolate

1 Grease and flour 2 baking trays or line with baking paper.

2 Place the butter in a small saucepan and heat gently until melted. Add the sugar, stir until dissolved, then bring the mixture to the boil. Remove from the heat and stir in the sultanas or raisins, cherries, ginger, sunflower seeds and almonds. Mix well, then beat in the cream.

3 Place small teaspoons of the fruit and nut mixture on to the prepared baking tray, allowing plenty of space for the mixture to spread out. Bake in a preheated oven, 180°C/350°F/Gas Mark 4, for 10–12 minutes or until they are a light golden colour.

4 Remove from the oven and, while still hot, use a circular biscuit cutter to pull in the edges to form perfect circles. Leave to cool and go crisp before removing from the baking tray.

5 Break the chocolate into pieces, place in a bowl and set over a saucepan of hot water. Stir until the chocolate has melted. Spread most of the chocolate on to a sheet of baking paper. When the chocolate is on the point of setting, place the biscuits flat-side down on the chocolate and leave to harden completely.

6 Cut around the florentines and remove from the baking paper. Spread a little more melted chocolate on the coated sides and use a fork to mark waves in the chocolate. Leave to set. Arrange the florentines on a plate with alternate sides facing upwards. Keep the florentines cool.

easy chocolate fudge

makes twenty-five pieces

500 g/1 lb 2 oz plain chocolate
75 g/2¾ oz unsalted butter
400 g/14 oz canned condensed milk
½ tsp vanilla essence

1 Lightly grease a 20-cm/8-inch square cake tin.

2 Break the chocolate into pieces and place in a large saucepan with the butter and condensed milk.

3 Heat gently, stirring until the chocolate and butter melts and the mixture is smooth. Do not allow the mixture to boil.

4 Remove from the heat. Beat in the vanilla essence, then beat the mixture for a few minutes until thickened. Pour it into the prepared tin and smooth the top.

5 Chill the mixture in the refrigerator until firm.

6 Tip the fudge out on to a chopping board and cut it into squares to serve.

COOK'S TIP

Store the fudge in an airtight container in a cool, dry place for up to 1 month. Do not freeze.

chocolate cherries

makes twenty-four

12 glacé cherries

2 tbsp rum or brandy

250 g/9 oz marzipan

125 g/4½ oz plain chocolate

extra milk, plain or white chocolate,

to decorate (optional)

VARIATION

Flatten the marzipan and use it to mould around the cherries to cover them, then dip in the chocolate as in main recipe.

1 Line a baking tray with a sheet of baking paper.

2 Cut the cherries in half and place in a small bowl. Add the rum or brandy and stir to coat. Leave the cherries to soak for at least 1 hour, stirring occasionally.

3 Divide the marzipan into 24 pieces and roll each piece into a ball. Press half a cherry into the top of each marzipan ball.

4 Break the chocolate into pieces, place in a bowl and set over a saucepan of hot water. Stir until it has melted.

5 Dip each sweet into the melted chocolate, using a cocktail stick, allowing the excess to drip back into the bowl. Place the coated cherries on the baking paper and chill until set.

6 If liked, melt a little extra chocolate and drizzle it over the top of the coated cherries. Leave to set.

cocochoc pyramids

makes twelve

150 ml/5 fl oz water

450 g/1 lb granulated sugar

pinch of cream of tartar

115 g/4 oz desiccated coconut

1 tbsp double cream

few drops of yellow food colouring

85 g/3 oz plain chocolate, broken

   into pieces

COOK'S TIP

For best results when cooking
with chocolate, always try to
use the best quality chocolate
that you can find.

1 Pour the water into a heavy-based saucepan, add the sugar and stir over a low heat until the sugar has dissolved. Stir in a pinch of cream of tartar and bring to the boil. Boil steadily, without stirring, until the temperature reaches 119°C/238°F on a sugar thermometer. If you do not have a sugar thermometer, test the syrup frequently by dropping a small quantity into a bowl of cold water. If the mixture can be rolled between your finger and thumb to make a soft ball, it is ready.

2 Remove the saucepan from the heat and beat in the coconut and cream. Continue to beat for 5–10 minutes, until the mixture becomes cloudy. Beat in a few drops of yellow food colouring, then leave to cool. When cool enough to handle, take small pieces of the mixture and form them into pyramids. Place the pyramids on a sheet of baking paper and leave to harden.

3 Put the chocolate into the top of a double boiler or in a heatproof bowl set over a saucepan of barely simmering water. Stir the chocolate over a low heat until melted, then remove it from the heat. Dip the bases of the pyramids into the melted chocolate and leave to set.

italian chocolate truffles

makes twenty-four

175 g/6 oz plain chocolate

2 tbsp Amaretto liqueur or orange-
flavoured liqueur

40 g/1½ oz unsalted butter

4 tbsp icing sugar

50 g/1¾ oz ground almonds

50 g/1¾ oz grated chocolate

VARIATION

Almond-flavoured liqueur gives
these truffles an authentic Italian
flavour. The original almond
liqueur, Amaretto di Saronno,
comes from Saronno in Italy.

1 Melt the chocolate with
the liqueur in a bowl set over a
saucepan of hot water, stirring
constantly until well combined.

2 Add the butter and stir until it
has melted. Stir in the icing
sugar and the ground almonds.

3 Leave the mixture in a cool
place until firm enough to roll
into about 24 balls.

4 Place the grated chocolate on
a plate and roll the truffles in
the chocolate to coat them.

5 Place the truffles in paper
sweet cases and chill.

white chocolate truffles

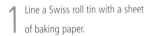

makes twenty

25 g/1 oz unsalted butter

5 tbsp double cream

225 g/8 oz good-quality Swiss
    white chocolate

1 tbsp orange-flavoured liqueur,
    optional

100 g/3½ oz white chocolate,
    to finish

1 Line a Swiss roll tin with a sheet of baking paper.

2 Place the butter and cream in a small saucepan and bring slowly to the boil, stirring constantly. Boil the butter and cream mixture for 1 minute, then remove from the heat.

3 Break the chocolate into pieces and add to the cream. Stir until melted, then beat in the liqueur (if using).

4 Pour into the prepared tin and chill for about 2 hours until firm.

5 Break off pieces of the truffle mixture and roll them into balls. Chill for a further 30 minutes before finishing the truffles.

6 To finish, melt the white chocolate in a bowl set over a saucepan of gently simmering water. Dip the balls in the melted chocolate, allowing the excess to drip back into the bowl. Place on non-stick baking paper and swirl the chocolate with the prongs of a fork. Leave the truffles to harden.

7 Drizzle a little melted plain chocolate over the truffles if you wish and leave to set. Place the truffles in paper cases to serve.

candied citrus peel

makes sixty

1 large unwaxed, thick-skinned
   orange

1 large unwaxed, thick-skinned
   lemon

1 large unwaxed, thick-skinned lime

600 g/1 lb 5 oz caster sugar

300 ml/10 fl oz water

125 g/4½ oz best-quality plain
   chocolate, chopped (optional)

1 Cut the orange into quarters lengthways and squeeze the juice into a cup to drink, or to use in another recipe. Cut each quarter in half lengthways to make 8 pieces.

2 Cut the fruit and pith away from the rind. If any of the pith remains on the rind, lay the knife almost flat on the white side of the rind and gently 'saw' backwards and forwards to slice it off because it will taste bitter.

3 Repeat with the lemon and lime, only cutting the lime into quarters. Cut each piece into 3 or 4 thin strips to make 60–80 strips in total. Place the strips in a saucepan of water and boil for 30 seconds. Drain thoroughly.

4 Dissolve the sugar in the water in a saucepan over a medium heat, stirring. Increase the heat and bring to the boil, without stirring. When the syrup becomes clear, turn the heat to its lowest setting.

5 Add the citrus strips, using a wooden spoon to push them in without stirring. Simmer in the syrup for 30 minutes, without stirring. Turn off the heat and set aside for at least 6 hours until completely cool.

6 Line a baking sheet with foil. Skim off the thin crust on top of the syrup without stirring. Remove the rind strips, one by one, from the syrup, shaking off any excess. Place the strips on the foil to cool.

7 To dip the candied peel in chocolate, melt the chocolate in a bowl set over a saucepan of gently simmering water. Working with one piece of candied peel at a time, dip the peel halfway into the chocolate. Return to the foil and leave to dry. Store in an airtight container.

chocolate eggnog

serves four

8 egg yolks

200 g/7 oz sugar

1 litre/1¾ pints milk

225 g/8 oz plain chocolate, grated

150 ml/5 fl oz dark rum

1 Beat the egg yolks with the sugar until thickened.

2 Pour the milk into a large saucepan, add the grated chocolate and bring to the boil. Remove from the heat and gradually beat in the egg yolk mixture. Stir in the rum and pour into heatproof glasses.

hot brandy chocolate

serves four

1 litre/1¾ pints milk

115 g/4 oz plain chocolate, broken
   into pieces

2 tbsp sugar

5 tbsp brandy

TO DECORATE

6 tbsp whipped cream

4 tsp cocoa powder, sifted

1 Pour the milk into a saucepan and bring to the boil, then remove from the heat. Place the chocolate in a small saucepan and add 2 tablespoons of the hot milk. Stir over a low heat until the chocolate has melted. Stir the chocolate mixture into the remaining milk and add the sugar.

2 Stir in the brandy and pour into 4 heatproof glasses. Top each with a swirl of whipped cream and sprinkle with a little cocoa powder.

cold chocolate drinks

serves two

CHOCOLATE MILK SHAKE

450 ml/16 fl oz ice-cold milk

3 tbsp drinking chocolate powder

3 scoops chocolate ice cream

cocoa powder, for dusting (optional)

CHOCOLATE ICE CREAM SODA

5 tbsp Glossy Chocolate Sauce (see
      page 104)

soda water

2 scoops chocolate ice cream

double cream, whipped

plain or milk chocolate, grated

1 To make the chocolate milk shake, place half of the ice-cold milk in a blender.

2 Add the drinking chocolate powder to the blender with 1 scoop of the chocolate ice cream. Blend until the mixture is frothy and well mixed. Stir in the remaining milk.

3 Place the remaining 2 scoops of chocolate ice cream in 2 tall serving glasses and carefully pour the chocolate milk over the scoops of chocolate ice cream.

4 Sprinkle a little cocoa powder (if using) over the top of each drink and serve immediately.

5 To make the chocolate ice cream soda, divide the Glossy Chocolate Sauce equally between two glasses.

6 Add a little soda water to each glass and stir to combine the sauce and soda water. Place a scoop of ice cream in each glass and then top up with more soda water.

7 Place a dollop of whipped double cream on the top, if liked, and sprinkle the soda with a little grated plain or milk chocolate.

COOK'S TIP

Served in a tall glass, a milk shake or an ice cream soda makes a scrumptious snack in a drink. Serve with straws, if wished.

A

almond
chocolate almond cake 10
chocolate & almond tart 152
chocolate & almond torte 46
chocolate pear & almond flan 73
& hazelnut gâteau 36
apple
chocolate apple pie 74
pancake stacks 78
apricot
chocolate & apricot squares 61
& chocolate ring 42

B

baked chocolate alaska 148
banana
chocolate & banana pancakes 70
chocolate banana sundae 122
coconut cheesecake 110
cream profiteroles 145
empanadas 94
biscotti, chocolate 191
bistvitny torte 44
black forest trifle 118
boxes
chocolate 221
raspberry chocolate 142
brandy
chocolate brandy torte 131
hot brandy chocolate 251
bread & butter pudding 68
bread pudding, chocolate 58
brownies
chocolate 206
chocolate fudge 176
bûche de nöel 56
butterfly cakes, chocolate 182

C

cakes
chocolate almond 10
chocolate & orange 14
chocolate & pineapple 12
chocolate & walnut 40
chocolate ganache 53
chocolate marshmallow 28
chocolate passion 22
chocolate slab 30
chocolate truffle 54
chocolate yogurt 23
date & chocolate 48

devil's food 18
family chocolate 13
mocha layer 16
mousse 31
no-bake refrigerator 52
rich chocolate layer 21
white truffle 50
candied citrus peel 248
cannoli 208
caramel squares, chocolate 194
caraque 7
cardamom cream horns 146
castle puddings, chocolate 99
champagne mousse 116
charlotte, chocolate 137
cheese pots, chocolate 114
cheesecakes
banana coconut 110
chocolate 128
marble 124
strawberry 130
chequerboard cookies 198
cherries, chocolate 243
chocolate
almond cake 10
& almond tart 152
& almond torte 46
apple pie 74
apricot & chocolate ring 42
& apricot squares 61
& banana pancakes 70
banana sundae 122
biscotti 191
boxes 221
brandy torte 131
bread pudding 58
brownie roulade 34
brownies 206
butterfly cakes 182
caramel squares 194
castle puddings 99
charlotte 137
cheese pots 114
cheesecake 128
cherries 243
& coconut cookies 210
& coconut roulade 33
coconut squares 186
cranberry sponge 98
crêpes 96
crispy bites 184
dairy wraps 180

date & chocolate cake 48
decorations 7
easy chocolate fudge 242
éclairs 188
eggnog 250
eve's pudding 67
family chocolate cake 13
fondue 79
freezer cake 134
french chocolate sauce 105
fried chocolate fingers 222
fruit crumble 69
fruit dip 102
fruit tartlets 126
fudge brownies 176
fudge pears 95
fudge pudding 75
fudge sauce 103
ganache cake 53
ginger puddings 64
glossy chocolate sauce 104
hazelnut palmiers 203
& hazelnut parfait 163
hazelnut pots 113
& honey ice cream 161
hot brandy chocolate 251
hot chocolate soufflé 84
ice cream soda 252
italian chocolate truffles 246
layer log 60
layered chocolate mousse 139
lemon chocolate pinwheels 218
liqueurs 226
malted chocolate wedges 196
marquise 120
marshmallow cake 28
marzipans 238
mascarpone cups 233
melting techniques 6
meringue pie 76
meringues 200
mexican chocolate meringues 201
milk shake 252
mini chocolate cones 236
mini chocolate tartlets 231
mint-chocolate gelato 164
mint swirl 121
mousse 136
no-bake chocolate squares 181
orange biscuits 193
& orange cake 14
orange sorbet 150

passion cake 22
pear & almond flan 73
pear tart 153
pecan pie 154–5
& pernod creams 171
& pineapple cake 12
pretzels 220
pudding with rum 89
queen of puddings 66
quick chocolate desserts 115
raspberry chocolate boxes 142
ravioli 80
rice dessert 166
rich chocolate ice cream 132
rich chocolate layer cake 21
roulade 32
rum babas 174
rum pots 112
saucy chocolate pudding 82
scones 183
shortcake towers 147
slab cake 30
sorbet 160
sticky chocolate puddings 90
teabread 20
tray bake 11
truffle cake 54
& vanilla creams 140
& vanilla loaf 51
viennese chocolate fingers 202
& walnut cake 40
yogurt cake 23
zabaglione 87
chocolate chip
cookies 213
flapjacks 212
muffins 190
tartlets 192
cocoa 4–5
cocochoc pyramids 244
coconut
banana coconut cheesecake 110
chocolate & coconut cookies 210
chocolate & coconut roulade 33
chocolate coconut squares 186
cocochoc pyramids 244
coffee sponge, steamed 88
cold desserts 106–71
collettes 237
cookies
chequerboard 198
chocolate & coconut 210

chocolate chip 213
cranberry sponge, chocolate 98
cream horns, cardamom 146
crêpes, chocolate 96
crispy bites, chocolate 184
crumble, chocolate fruit 69
curls, quick 7

D
dairy wraps, chocolate 180
dark & white chocolate torte 43
date & chocolate cake 48
decorations 7
desserts
cold 106–71
hot 62–105
devil's food cake 18
dobos torte 41
drinks 250–2
dutch macaroons 211

E
easy chocolate fudge 242
éclairs, chocolate 188
eggnog, chocolate 250
empanadas, banana 94
eve's pudding, chocolate 67

F
family chocolate cake 13
filo nests 170
flapjacks, chocolate chip 212
florentines 216
florentines, mini 240
fondue, chocolate 79
freezer cake, chocolate 134
french chocolate sauce 105
fried chocolate fingers 222
fruit
chocolate fruit crumble 69
chocolate fruit dip 102
chocolate fruit tartlets 126
& nut fudge 229
tropical fruit kebabs 92
fudge
easy chocolate 242
fruit & nut 229
fudge pudding 86

G
gâteaux
almond & hazelnut 36

layered meringue 38
ginger puddings, chocolate 64
glossy chocolate sauce 104

H
hazelnut
almond & hazelnut gâteau 36
chocolate & hazelnut parfait 163
chocolate hazelnut palmiers 203
chocolate hazelnut pots 113
hot brandy chocolate 251
hot chocolate soufflé 84
hot desserts 62–105

I
ice cream
chocolate & honey 161
italian drowned 100
marshmallow 162
mint-chocolate gelato 164
rich chocolate 132
white chocolate 123
ice cream soda, chocolate 252
iced white chocolate terrine 108
italian chocolate truffles 246
italian drowned ice cream 100

L
layered chocolate mousse 139
layered meringue gâteau 38
leaves 7
lemon chocolate pinwheels 218
liqueurs, chocolate 226
log, chocolate layer 60

M
macaroons, dutch 211
malted chocolate wedges 196
marble cheesecake 124
marquise, chocolate 120
marshmallow
chocolate marshmallow cake 28
ice cream 162
marzipans, chocolate 238
mascarpone cups, chocolate 233
melting techniques 6
meringue
baked chocolate alaska 148
chocolate meringue pie 76
chocolate meringues 200
fingers 223
layered meringue gâteau 38

mexican chocolate meringues 201
raspberry vacherin 24
mexican chocolate meringues 201
milk shake, chocolate 252
millionaire's shortbread 214
mini chocolate cones 236
mini chocolate tartlets 231
mini florentines 240
mint
  chocolate mint swirl 121
  mint-chocolate gelato 164
mississippi mud pie 156
mocha
  creams 144
  layer cake 16
  swirl mousse 138
mousse
  champagne 116
  chocolate 136
  layered chocolate 139
  mocha swirl 138
mousse cake 31
muffins, chocolate chip 190

N

nectarines, stuffed 93
no-bake chocolate squares 181
no-bake refrigerator cake 52
nutty chocolate clusters 228

O

orange
  chocolate & orange cake 14
  chocolate orange biscuits 193
  chocolate orange sorbet 150

P

pain au chocolat 178
pancakes
  apple pancake stacks 78
  chocolate & banana 70
passion cake, chocolate 22
pear
  chocolate fudge pears 95
  chocolate pear & almond flan 73
  chocolate pear tart 153
  poached in chocolate 72
pecan
  chocolate pecan pie 154–5
  fudge ring 83
pineapple cake, chocolate & 12
poached pears in chocolate 72

pretzels, chocolate 220
profiteroles, banana cream 145

Q

queen of puddings, chocolate 66
quick chocolate desserts 115
quick curls 7

R

raspberry
  chocolate boxes 142
  vacherin 24
ravioli, chocolate 80
rice dessert, chocolate 166
rice pudding tartlets 204
rich chocolate ice cream 132
rich chocolate layer cake 21
rocky road bites 232
roulades
  chocolate 32
  chocolate & coconut 33
  chocolate brownie 34
rum
  chocolate pudding with 89
  chocolate rum babas 174
  chocolate rum pots 112
  truffles 234

S

sachertorte 26
sauces
  chocolate fudge 103
  french chocolate 105
  glossy chocolate 104
saucy chocolate pudding 82
scones, chocolate 183
shortcake towers, chocolate 147
sorbets
  chocolate 160
  chocolate orange 150
soufflé, hot chocolate 84
steamed coffee sponge 88
sticky chocolate puddings 90
strawberry cheesecake 130
stuffed nectarines 93
sweets 224–49

T

teabread, chocolate 20
tiramisu layers 129
tortes
  bistvitny 44

chocolate & almond 46
chocolate brandy 131
dark & white chocolate 43
dobos 41
tray bake, chocolate 11
trifle, black forest 118
tropical fruit kebabs 92
truffles
  italian chocolate 246
  rum 234
  white chocolate 247

V

viennese chocolate fingers 202

W

walnut cake, chocolate & 40
white chocolate
  dark & white chocolate torte 43
  ice cream 123
  iced terrine 108
  moulds 158
  truffles 247
white truffle cake 50

Z

zabaglione, chocolate 87
zuccherini 169
zuccotto 168